3·50 +

D1461623

WITHDRAWN
FROM STOCK

ON CAPITALIST UNDERDEVELOPMENT

ON CAPITALIST UNDERDEVELOPMENT

ANDRE GUNDER FRANK

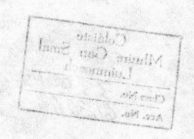

Bombay
OXFORD UNIVERSITY PRESS
Delhi   Calcutta   Madras

Oxford University Press

Oxford London Glasgow
New York Toronto Melbourne Auckland
Kuala Lumpur Singapore Hong Kong Tokyo
Delhi Bombay Calcutta Madras Karachi
Nairobi Dar es Salaam Cape Town
and associates in
Beirut Berlin Ibadan Mexico City Nicosia

André Gunder FRANK 1929

First published 1975
Reprinted 1976, 1979, 1982

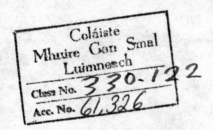
Printed by C. S. Ubhayaker, Ubsons Printers, Hammersmith
Industrial Estate, Mahim, Bombay-400 016 and published by
R. Dayal, Oxford University Press, Oxford House, Apollo Bunder,
Bombay-400 039.

Contents

Preface

This essay was written during October-November 1963, in Rio de Janeiro, Brazil. As I recall, it was then read by one person only; and during the six years it has lain in first draft manuscript form in my files, even I forgot what this essay was about. Since I am now preparing another work on underdevelopment, I took the manuscript out of the files to see what references or ideas it might contain that could help me in my present task. I did not find many references (and some that appear in the manuscript I cannot now trace) but I did find more ideas, albeit often rather speculative ones, than I expected. Some of these ideas in the manuscript, I now see, must also have remained in my head; because they appear in more developed or at least more documented form in later writings: the chain between metropole and periphery became the model for my 1964 study on the underdevelopment of Chile; the questions posed about internal colonialism were in part answered in my 1965 study on Brazil and my 1964-5 essay on the Indian problem — all of which have since been published as part of my book *Capitalism and Underdevelopment in Latin America* (1967-71); and the conception of the dialectical unity between the development of the development and the development of the underdevelopment guided all these essays and many other later ones, especially the one entitled 'The Development of Underdevelopment'.

But until I re-read this early manuscript I had not realized what raw material or at least raw ideas were already in this essay—nor that it contained some which I had forgotten and never reworked since. But in this essay they formed a part of a coherent whole, some of which have borne fruit through my later studies and some of which might conceivably bear fruit through other minds that may only just be beginning to devote themselves to the study of under-development.

For this reason, I have decided to prepare this essay for publication. I have left the essay as it was originally written. To do otherwise would mean — after years of further study — to prepare a

viii

completely different work. This is in fact being done, since I am in the process of completing two years of work with Said Ahmad Shah on a two-volume 1,500 page anthology on Asia, Africa and Latin America, entitled *Underdevelopment: History, Theory, Policy, Politics.* Therefore, the changes I have now made in the original essay are limited only to improvements of grammar and corrections of spelling (since the manuscript had not even been proof-read), to the elimination of some, but by no means all, repetitions, and to the occasional addition of dates or disagreements in parentheses. I have even left the speculative, almost stream of conciousness — and often cumbersome — style and beg the reader to forgive me. The only major change I have now made is the following: This essay began as a critique of the conventional wisdom, especially in the sociology of development, but then veered off to speculate about an alternative approach to the study of development and underdevelopment. The critical references to specific other theories of development were later expanded and published under the title *Sociology of Development and Underdevelopment of Sociology,* and other essays now collected in *Latin America: Underdevelopment or Revolution,* (Monthly Review Press 1969); and these references have now been eliminated from the present essay (although some ideas retained here about liberalism and functionalism were also incorporated in later sociological essays). Some theoretical and political formulations, especially about class, I would not make in the same way today, but I also leave them as they were then. In a word, I am now offering this essay as it was written six years ago, for whatever worth, if any, it may still have.

Finally and belatedly, I should like to acknowledge the aid of Messrs. Manual Diegues Jr., Director, and Rodolfo Stavenhagen, then Secretary General, of the Centro Latino-Americano de Pesquisas em Ciencias Sociais in Rio de Janeiro, where this essay was written.

Santiago de Chile
October 1, 1969

A.G.F.

Addition to the Preface

The present book was written at the very beginning of the ascent of the 'dependence theory' as an interpretation of underdevelopment in Latin America and elsewhere, and this book represents an early statement of the theory and a simple application of the approach to a series of problems, e.g. critique of previously received theory, history, imperialism, internal colonialism, exploitation, class, socialism and liberation. The word 'on' in the book's title reflects the introductory and provisional nature of the book's presentation and argument.

Nonetheless, at the time of preparing this book for publication and writing the preface above in 1969 no concise and general introduction and application of the 'dependence theory' had yet been published in book form. This lack has since been remedied, albeit from differing political perspectives, by Fernando Henrique Cardoso, Theotonio dos Santos, Osvaldo Sunkel and others. Moreover, the 'dependence' approach has since then — in my opinion and that of an increasing number of others — ripened to maturity at least in Latin America.

The work on the theoretical introduction of the above mentioned anthology has during the past two years led me to the preparation of a separate new book, provisionally entitled *Accumulating Exploitation*, (London, Penguin Books, in press). Although this new book and the present one deal with the same problems — capitalist underdevelopment — they approach it in different ways.

The new book differs from the present one to begin with in that it is written — in 1970 and 1971, already after the decade of the 1960's — at a time when the advance of the 'dependence theory' has already come to a halt after having given all it had to give, at least in Latin America though perhaps not elsewhere. While the above mentioned still unpublished anthology on underdevelopment is still intended to extend the 'dependence' approach to the study of underdevelopment outside Latin America, the new book (though it began as an 'introduction' to the latter) is then dedicated to over-- coming the limitations of 'dependence' and to go beyond it to parti- cipate in the forging of a more adequate approach to the analysis and elimination of underdevelopment. In the development of this 'new' — in quotation marks because it had been classical from Smith to Marx — analysis of the process of capital accumulation, new pioneering contributions have already been made by Amin* Palloix*, Arrighi*, Hinkelammert*, Marini*, and others.

Our new book only attempts to inquire what function the various new underdeveloped regions of the world had in each stage and at several moments of the historical process of world capital accu- mulation and how this global function was and is economically and politically related to the peculiarities of accumulation in these regions themselves. This is not to say that we now reject the 'depend- ence' approach as incorrect. On the contrary, we still believe that compared to literally neo-classical economic, social and political theory the development of 'dependence' in the 1960's represented an important departure and advance in the study of the under- developed world.

But we now also recognize that reliance on 'dependence' involves certain limitations in the analysis of the internal dynamics of the metropolis, of the satellites and of course of the world capitalist system as a whole. It is because of our desire to share this awareness with the reader and to alert him to this limitation of 'dependence' *per se* (beyond the obvious limitations of this introductory book) that this additional preface is written prior to the publication of the present book.

Santiago de Chile   A.G.F.
August 15, 1971

* See Bibliography

1

On Development and Underdevelopment

UNDERDEVELOPMENT is not just the lack of development. Before there was development there was no underdevelopment. This relation between development and underdevelopment is not just a comparative one, in the sense that some places are more developed or underdeveloped than others: development and underdevelopment are also related, both through the common historical process that they have shared during the past several centuries and through the mutual, that is reciprocal, influence that they have had, still have, and will continue to have, on each other throughout history.

This paper will outline the history of how underdevelopment in fact developed; it will demonstrate that underdevelopment developed in intimate relation with the development of the now-developed countries as simultaneous results of the historical process of capitalist development over the past centuries, and finally attempt to indicate some elements of an interpretative, that is a theoretical, approach to the analysis, understanding, and intentional *transformation* of this still continuing trend toward ever growing development and *growing underdevelopment*.

Colonization and Underdevelopment

In his excellént little book on *Les Pays Sous-Développés*, Yves Lacoste notes 'the underdeveloped countries cannot be understood if one abstracts from foreign influence' (Lacoste 1961, p. 83),* and 'underdevelopment results fundamentally from the intrusion of the capitalist system...' (ibid. p. 79). Nonetheless, a couple of

* For references see Bibliography on p. 111.

pages earlier he argues, '. . . in spite of the fact that a large part
of these causes (of underdevelopment) are due to the fact of colonialism, underdevelopment is a different phenomenon.' (ibid. p. 76)
If in our days colony and underdevelopment coincide, for a long time
(from the 16th to the end of the 19th century) the colonial dominions
still were not characterized by underdevelopment: they were still
anticipating its appearance. They displayed, then, aspects of a relatively equilibrated system. . .' (ibid. p. 76). He explains on an earlier
page (ibid. p. 54), 'the present state of the underdeveloped countries,
from the economic as well as from the social point of view, comes from
the rise in England at the end of the 18th century of this complex
phenomenon called "the industrial revolution." He concludes, 'In
fact, in time and space, colonization and underdevelopment are not
superimposed exactly. . . not all colonized countries became underdeveloped (U.S.A., Australia, etc.) nor were all underdeveloped
countries colonies (Southern Europe, Japan),' (ibid. p. 76). Though I
can only recommend Lacoste's book as one of the best existing intro-
ductions or summaries to underdevelopment, I cannot agree that his
above quoted argument, is acceptable.

The facts nonetheless force upon us the conclusion that underdevelopment is systematically and everywhere associated with—
in fact caused by—colonization. The word 'colony' and its various
derivatives like 'colonization' and 'colonialism' received a special
somewhat restricted meaning derived from the particular experience
of the 16th-17th century and again of the 19th century colonial
waves: reflecting these experiences, the concept came to connote
among other things, physical and political occupation and domination, as well as a certain dominant, determinant/subordinate,
exploitative relation. But the fact that we can now speak of 'neo-
colonialism' and refer to an essentially similar relation which does
not include formal political incorporation, suggests that 'colonial'
also has a wider meaning and essence. The fact that 'colonialism'
and 'imperialism' have been used, especially in reference to certain
phenomena of the period 1870-1960, almost interchangeably, and
that 'imperialism' is derived from 'empire' or 'imperial system',
suggests that the colony, by common understanding, is the domi-
nated part of a system in which the imperialist is the domineering
part. In short, 'colonial', 'imperial', and 'capitalist' all refer to a
set of relationships, and more importantly as a *system* of relations,

in which domination, super-subordination, exploitation, and of course, development and underdevelopment, play a central part. I shall suggest below that, furthermore, they must all be understood to refer to the same system which may be described by the phenomenon they all have in common, might best be called 'capitalist'.

To return to the facts, we may rely on the Marquis de Pombal, the Portuguese Colbert, as a guide. Writing as early as in 1755 he noted that

> 'The Portuguese Monarchy was at its last gasp. The English had firmly bound the nation in a state of dependence. They had conquered it without the inconvenience of a conquest... Portugal was powerless and without vigor, and all her movements were regulated by the desires of England...In 1754 Portugal scarcely produced anything towards her own support. Two thirds of her physical necessities were supplied by England... England had become mistress of the entire commerce of Portugal, all the trade of the country was carried by her agents. The English were at the same time furnishers and the retailers of all the necessities of life that the country required. Having a monopoly of everything, no business was carried on but through their hands...The English came to Lisbon to monopolize even the commerce of Brazil...The foreigners after having acquired immense fortunes disappeared on a sudden, carrying with them the riches of the country. '(Manchester 1933, p. 39).

Yet, many years later Ricardo and his followers illustrated their supposed 'law of comparative advantage' with the example of trade between England and Portugal: Portugal should produce wine while England produces textiles. However, not only do changes in products produce changes in resources, but not all products are the same, especially in their effects on resources and productive capacity. We now know that producing textiles augments industrial capacity while producing wine, as Portugal learned to its dismay, produces agricultural capacity. England industrialized; Portugal didn't. But since Ricardo was talking about comparative and not absolute advantage, each country had to have a productive capacity in both goods for the theory to be relevant at all. Well, I don't know if England produced wine. But Portugal had been producing textiles. Thanks to Ricardian type policy, incorporated into the Treaty of Methuen and three earlier Anglo-Portuguese trade agreements, Portugal de-industrialized, that is to say became more underdeveloped, while the opposite happened in England.

The matter is still worse however. Ricardo's theory assumes there are only two industries—wine and textiles. He assumes that exchange, that is trade, is costless and without direct benefit. But it isn't. All the wine-textile trade, not only transport, but finance, merchandizing, everything connected with the trade was in the hands of the British. They cleaned out the Portuguese lock, stock, and wine-barrel in Portugal and in Brazil. (It is noteworthy to mark the dates of all this. The Treaty of Methuen was in 1703. The earlier trade agreements responsible for the cumulative power of England over Portugal date from 1647 and Ricardo's theory from 1817).

It can, and should, reasonably be maintained that the result was not only a comparatively lower level of development in Portugal than in England, but the development of much of what we would today call the structure of underdevelopment. It is undoubtedly true, as Lacoste suggests, that some contemporary features of underdevelopment developed at a later time. But so did those of development. The entire system is continually transforming itself and changing some of its manifestations. But in addition to distinguishing among differences it is also important to recognize similarities and, as I suggest there are, an indentity of fundamental constituents. It is probably incorrect to assume as Lacoste does that, all the features of underdevelopment are new and derived from the industrial revolution—a question to which we shall have to return in reference to Marxist interpretations. Certainly Pombal would not have agreed with Lacoste that he was not talking about what today we call underdevelopment.

The remainder of Southern Europe and Portugal since Pombal's time, which by Lacoste's classification and general agreement are termed 'underdeveloped' must be handled in the same way. They were most definitely colonized and can in no way, be taken to constitute exceptions to the correlation, which I suggest is perfect and which Lacoste thinks is only almost so. To jump ahead, but here Lacoste and I are again in agreement, the 'Mezzaggiorno' in the South of Italy and the 'Old' South of the United States equally well fit the pattern to cover part of the relation—though only partly since they were also 'colonized' by the outside—we may have to introduce the term 'internal colonization' which already has some currency elsewhere. (Gonzales Casanova, 1963).

Lacoste, quite rightly included Eastern Europe in both his 'under-developed' and 'colonial' group. I might add Ireland, as Marx already did. So there is no argument there. But curiously, Lacoste makes special note of the fact that in Eastern Europe (and we again add Ireland) ethnic problems are severe and the states are relatively young *in spite of very strong nationalism.* The nationalism of Eastern Europe must be understood, precisely as the product of and reaction to that domination and exploitation. As such, the 19th century nationalism of Eastern Europe was fundamentally different from that of 19th century Western Europe. The one was the nation-alism, especially after 1870, fanned by the right-wing exploiters and the other that of the relatively progressive leaders of the exploited. The nationalism of the underdeveloped world today is, of course, the nationalism of the 'eastern', not of the 'western' type. Little wonder that the West now claims that the time for nationalism has long since passed, that the time has come for unity (under whose leadership?). We shall have to return later to the question of how progressive this nationalism really is in the hands of the national bourgeoisie.

Lacoste calls Japan the only industrialized country among the underdeveloped ones. If Japan is industrialized that is due precisely to the fact that it was never colonized in the sense that other countries were. Japan is the unique and most instructive case of a country whose ruling class decided to develop the country and to do so before it might become incorporated into the colonialist-imperialist-capitalist system in the usual way. In fact, there were of course also domestic circumstances which made this step propi-tious. The Japanese looked across the water to see what was already happening to China where, to use a later term for a somewhat earlier period, the door was being opened to the foreigners and the Japanese learned a lesson: they decided to go it alone without foreign 'investment' and 'aid'. Since it was the people who were already in power who decided to industrialize the country, they did not first have to make a revolution, much less a revolution against a ruling group which is not only entrenched and conser-vative but allied to a foreign centre of power whose effective interests are to keep the country from developing as well.

It is curious, but not really surprising, that given the very great amount of scientific attention Japan's development attracts compared to the attention the non-development of China has received, practically no one in the West (excepting Norman, 1940 and Baran, 1957) has observed this crucial distinction between Japan and other countries: Japan did not get caught in the imperialist system 'initially'. She may have been *un*-developed in 1868, but she was not *under*-developed; and that is why she was able, by her own efforts, to develop. If Japan has not managed 'fully' to develop since, if Lacoste is right in classifying her among the underdeveloped (in terms of an unacceptable definition of that term as *relative* per capita income) that lends only further evidence to my argument. For now the relevant comparison is with the Soviet Union. Both went it alone in their development efforts. The U.S.S.R. made it, or, everyone concedes, will make it (after an approximately equal period of time since their respective development efforts began). By 1905, with both countries capitalist but Japan going it alone while Russia was receiving foreign 'help', Japan, as her war with Russia proved, was way ahead. In our time, or even in (for them) pre-war 1941, the U.S.S.R. must be put way ahead despite the fact that in terms of output she had stood still (or rather fallen back and recovered) between 1913 and 1928.

But there was another difference: the U.S.S.R. had changed from capitalism to socialism. This did make a difference. But the fact that Japan began with (though significantly, as noted, on her own rather than being incorporated into) capitalism and remained under capitalism has also had its inevitable consequences—it has in the long run caught her up in the imperialist system anyway. By becoming capitalist and expanding, she became an imperialist power herself. Being an imperialist power she came into conflict with other imperialist powers—and was defeated. Now foreign capital *is*, since World War II, entering Japan. Though originally independently capitalist, she inevitably became involved in the ultimately *single* capitalist system. Since Japan had not developed far enough—away from *un*development rather than *under*development—not to find herself still at a relative disadvantage in the face of the more powerful participants in the system, Lacoste may be partly right in calling Japan underdeveloped: she may be acquiring some of the features of underdevelopment after all.

The Soviet Union, socialist though it is, has also not been able to extricate herself completely from the capitalist-imperialist system.

Had she been able to do so, that is, had she not had to fight a defensive action in the counter-revolutionary war of 1920, the Second World War of 1941 and the Cold War, she would, no one can doubt it, be far more developed today than she is. In short, the conclusion is inescapable, Lacoste's minor objection to the contrary notwithstanding, without exception, every single one of the countries that are by common agreement classified as underdeveloped have had a colonial position within the world capitalist system. Most continue in a colonial or neo-colonial position and remain underdeveloped, indeed continue to underdevelop ever more. The others escaped the system by turning socialist and appear to be on the way to development.

The evidence also compels the conclusion that the colonized countries are underdeveloped. Lacoste raises the obvious objection that the United States, Australia, etc., and I might add Israel and maybe even South Africa which he probably did not have in mind, are developed. That is not to be denied, with obvious reservations for the two countries I added. But if the evidence of colonization is properly interpreted (not 'properly' to fit a procrustian theory but 'properly' to distil out its proper substance) then the evidence lends still further confirmation to the hypothesis that underdevelopment and colonialism are perfectly correlated in both directions. The question arises, what in colonization is really significant for underdevelopment? To answer this question I propose a slight detour.

In certain circles it is claimed that most of the capital around the capitalist world is owned by Jews, that there is a Jewish conspiracy, and that this is the source of all our troubles. (This is not an anticapitalist movement, of course. On the contrary, more recently it has become fashionable in part of these circles to say that the conspiracy is really a Jewish-Communist one, witness that all the top Soviet leaders are Jewish, some of them having significantly changed their names to obscure this nonetheless clear situation). Well, for all I know a goodly part of capital really may be owned or controlled by Jews. But I also know that there is no Jewish conspiracy among them to use that capital to the benefit of Jews and the disbenefit of non-Jews. And that is critical, for it may also be possible that a very large part of capital is really controlled by blue-eyed people. Sergio Bagú supplied an example of the significance of this consideration in the 15th century already. The Iberian Peninsula was inhabited at the

time, among others, by Moors and Jews. The Moors had important
technical agricultural skills and it may be claimed were the local
representatives of an empire which had for some time been colonizing
the Peninsula. The Jews owned capital. The year 1492 saw, among
other interesting events such as the union of Castilla and Aragon and
the discovery of a new continent by one Columbus, of the expulsion
from Spain of the Moors and the Jews. The Moors took their agricultural skills with them, and that was bad for Spanish agriculture. But
it carried with it the compensation, one might claim, of liberating
Spain from a foreign dominating power(s) to which it was paying
tribute, etc. The Jews took with them their capital. That was bad for
Spanish economy too. But what was the compensation? Had they
been using their capital for the benefit of Jews (particularly elsewhere)
and to the detriment of the Spanish economy before they left? No,
quite the opposite. They had made Spain much of the trading power
that she was when she undertook to discover and colonize America.
But after being expelled, the Jews really did take their capital out—
and put it to work expanding the commercial power of Spain's
European rivals, the same ones who ultimately sealed her doom. I
think the moral we should draw is clear. Is Israel really colonizing
the United States?

Did Great Britain colonize the United States? It did in at least
one way—it sent 'colonists' there who with the capital they brought
along developed a national economy with national interests separate
from that of those who stayed at home. They were able to separate
the United States and develop it separately as they never could
have, history suggests, if they had been a colony like South America
or the West Indies. They did not, to be sure, develop the country
for the benefit of the indigenous inhabitants any more than did the
Australians for their aborigines, the white South Africans for the
'initial' (but not previously underdeveloped!) Africans or the Israeli
Jews for the Palestinian Arabs. The immigrant colonists developed
the country for themselves, themselves colonizing and exploiting
the indigenous inhabitants where possible as in South Africa, or
killing them off as in America, or kicking them out as in Israel.

In the United States and the Dominions, in short, capital and
colonist came jointly, and both went to work there, as had the Jews
and their capital in Spain. Pombal understood that not political
conquest but economic conquest is the essence of colonialism. The

same may be said for political independence and economic independence, then or now, though of course more often than not the two are, however formally separate, effectively joined. The evidence from the United States and the Dominions, fortifies the inference that being an economic colony under capitalism produces underdevelopment. In fact, history provides not one case of a country which has received substantial foreign investment (in which the capital remained effectively foreign and was not accompanied by colonists) which is today generally conceded to be developed, much less which has changed from the generally accepted category of underdeveloped to that of developed—under capitalism. The Soviet Union did manage to develop despite being subject to foreign 'aid' in earlier years, but only by turning socialist and cutting off that 'aid'. Several contemporary countries have, of course, recently tried to extricate themselves from the imperialist system and to develop under 'national capitalism', either with or without 'aid', but none of them, notably India, Egypt or Brazil, have succeeded. It may be interesting to speculate whether an ex-colonial socialist country which receives aid from capitalist ones, or a socialist one which receives aid from socialist ones, can succeed in escaping underdevelopment. The period for which history supplies evidence is perhaps still too short for any conclusive answer. Of the first, capitalist to socialist aid, there is only one case, Yugoslavia. It has so far (1963) had a highly satisfactory growth rate well distributed among its regions. That has now declined, maybe temporarily, maybe not. But the question arises as to whether it is even still socialist or whether, thanks in part to the aid, it has been sucked back into the capitalist system — and whether it can thereby escape underdevelopment. So argue, of course, the Chinese (cf. *Peking Review*, 1963, Is Yugoslavia a Socialist Country?). As for socialist to socialist aid, the evidence is not available though several theories are.

Development of the Developed

Let us turn to some matters concerning development. It will not be possible, of course, to attempt here a history or analysis of the process of development and its variations. I wish to limit the discussion to the 'contribution' to the development of developed areas made by the now underdeveloped ones. Even within this limited topic, I cannot attempt a history, a survey, or an evaluation of this contribution, if any, but will merely suggest some more or less technical considerations of which any satisfactory analysis of that contribution would have to take account.

In assessing the past, in terms of the actual, or potential contribution of a now relatively poor and underdeveloped area to a relatively rich developed one, it will not do at all to talk in the static global, undiscriminating terms of suggesting, as so often happens, that the poor are so numerous that redistributing wealth (or income) to them from the rich only 'equalizes or spreads the poverty', or that the rich are so rich that a transfer of resources to them from the poor who have so little to give up hardly helps the rich in any significant way. Instead, it will be necessary to examine four other factors, at least, that are crucial to an assessment of the contribution made by the underdeveloped to the developed: (1) the economic 'surplus' and the role it plays in capital accumulation; (2) the inefficiency or wastefulness of spoilation or exploitation and the resulting possibility that sacrifice exceeds contribution; (3) the discontinuities over time in the development of development and/or underdevelopment, and the possible importance of a marginal but qualitatively important upward or downward push at a critical point in time; and (4) organizational or market discontinuities, such as monopoly, and the possibility that a contribution to a part is greater than to its whole: Finally, there is the further consideration — we might number it the fifth though it encompasses all the rest — of contribution to system maintenance as a whole or, to use Talcott Parsons' term, 'latent pattern maintenance'. Here, I can do little more than suggest the significance of these considerations.

Surplus

Economic surplus is critical for economic development and underdevelopment. Similarly, our understanding of development and underdevelopment depends heavily on the use of the concept 'economic surplus'. The idea of surplus already played a key role in the analysis of Marx. As Celso Furtado (1961: pp. 37-8) points out the criticism of Marx's labour and surplus based theory of value

since Boehm-Bawerk — and one might add choUSED by all margi-
nalists ever since — is largely beside the point. They are concerned
to explain the harmonic equilibration of a given system at a point
in time. Marx was, and we are, concerned with understanding
development — and underdevelopment. And 'economic surplus'
may be called the actual or potential excess of a social unit's production over its necessary consumption which may or may not be
exploited or invested. The fact that there are unquestionably serious
conceptual and measurement difficulties, summarised, for instance
by Baran (1957), which surround the concept of economic surplus is
not critically relevant for present purposes. The same might be
said with respect to 'national income' and any number of other
economic, social, and political categories in current use.

The importance of the economic surplus for development — and
underdevelopment — is what is done with it. Among anthropolo-
gists, the neo-whiteans have argued that the entire stratification
system of a society, is based on the appropriation of the surplus.
In some societies the upper reaches, or those somewhat below, of
the stratification system, who live thanks to their appropriation of
the surplus, also use it to create high culture — or development.
See for instance Marvin Harris (1959), Marshall Sahlins (1958,)
Paul Baran (1957), who may be credited with (re?) popularizing
the concept among some of our contemporaries, have argued effectively that it is not so much the total wealth or income of a society,
but its surplus and the way it is used which determines the kind and
type of development or underdevelopment that occurs. Raúl Prebisch, while still head of CEPAL (ECLA) began to insist that the
'spreading the poverty' argument is quite irrelevant for the problem
of development which turns on the extent and direction of investment of the surplus which is now appropriated by the upper income
groups for consumption. (The most recent (1963) and maybe fullest
statement of his argument may be found perhaps in Prebisch's 'last
report' before retiring, delivered at Mar del Plata, Argentina, in
May 1963 under the little 'Towards a Dynamic of Latin American
Development'). Prebisch there calculates that if the upper income
earners were to reduce their income from the current 15 times to
only 11 times the income of the lowest group, the growth rate of per
capita national income could be raised from the current 1% to 3%
per annum. A further fall to 9 times the income of the lowest group

would release enough of the surplus to raise the growth rate by another 1% to 4% per capita. It should be noted, however, that in his calculations Prebisch is referring only to the part of the actual surplus which is actually being received by the upper income recipients. The more relevant surplus which includes the Latin America income now received by foreigners and exported abroad, and the still larger portion which is not received at all but wasted, is of course much larger and represents a much greater development and underdevelopment potential.

For purposes of development and underdevelopment, it is not, then, so much the sacrifice in the loser country of wealth or income or its contribution to the gainer country as it is the sacrifice of and contribution to surplus that is critical. There has been a long-standing debate about colonialism/imperialism in general and about each colonial/imperialized country and period in particular as to just how much they have lost (and gained) through colonialism/imperialism. The debate has been even more intensive with respect to how much the 'mother' or metropolitan countries have gained. There is of course more agreement on the colonies having lost than on the colonizers having gained. A review of this whole literature cannot be undertaken here, nor does it have to, since much of it is largely irrelevant to our problem since it deals with total and not with *surplus* income. This reservation must be made, for instance, with respect to much of the several chapter discussion which John Strachey (1959) pursues under the title 'Are the Empires Profitable?'. This same objection, among several others, must also be raised against the contemporary argument that the United States cannot possibly be exploiting other economies such as those of Latin America because after all U.S. foreign trade put together only represents 3% of her G.N.P. In short, despite the already existing vast literature on the contribution of Latin American riches to Spain, Portugal and the rest of Western Europe, and thereby later also to its overseas off-shoots like the U.S., or of India and other parts of the Empire to Britain, etc., much of the evaluation of the real contribution to the developing economies' fund of surplus, that is of investment, remains still to be done. I suspect that this contribution was not only large, but crucial — for additional reasons still to be seen below.

However great the contribution to metropolitan development may or may not be, the associated sacrifice in terms of underdevelopment can readily be greater. I do not think we need very refined measurements to be sure that this is, has been, and continues to be so. On this point Strachey is quite clear, and he attributes it to the incredible and wasteful spoilation of the initial colonization. Everyone who has examined the conquest of Latin America, India, Africa, the Middle East or any other place has undoubtedly noted that the gain and contribution to the winner is probably not nearly commensurate with the terrible sacrifice to the loser. But of course the conqueror need not care that for him to gain a pound of flesh his victim is losing 100 — or, indeed, his life, as when whole civilizations were destroyed or at least lost their lifeblood as when essential irrigation systems were forced into disuse.

But development and underdevelopment are not the summation only of economic quantities. They are their cumulation and the whole social structure and process which determines that accumulation. Equally important to the 'initial' contribution and sacrifice is this cumulative one. However important the cumulative contribution of colonialism-capitalism-imperialism may or may not have been, it is quite clear that the now underdeveloped countries' participation in that capitalist system has undoubtedly made a — perhaps the — most important contribution to their underdevelopment.

This contribution of imperialism and capitalism to the underdevelopment of underdeveloped areas continues in our own day. It is not, of course, so much the resources that the United States draws out of South Korea, or South Vietnam, or South America as it is the employ of America's economic, political, social, cultural, and of course above all armed force to maintain these countries' economic, political, social, cultural, and of course military structure of underdevelopment. This structure imposes on them the greatest sacrifice, the sacrifice of production foregone, of their infant children's — and their war torn populations' — lives foregone, of their culture (past and future) foregone, of their freedom foregone, the future development possibilities foregone by their forced ever deeper underdevelopment today. All for what, we may ask? To prevent the development of their economy, society, and culture as in North Korea, North Vietnam, and Cuba? The capitalist system may be a positive sum game in which some players however gain so much and others lose so much that at the time of the present deal and after centuries of play the losers have absolutely and not only relatively less than they started with; or it may for all we know even be a negative sum game in which, precisely the winners have won less than the losers lost, but there is certainly no reason to think that it is a zero sum game or a positive sum game in which both winner and loser have gained at least an absolutely greater share of the original pot or pie.

Alfred Marshal was most certainly wrong in telling us that *natura non facit saltum** and in assembling a whole 'engine of analysis', as Milton Friedman likes to call it, around this central but erroneous conception of the world. A third consideration for the evaluation of the contribution of the colonial imperialist, that is capitalist, relationship to the development of development and the development of underdevelopment is discontinuity, or 'jump' as Marshal called it. As Leibenstein popularized with his 'low level equilibrium trap', and Rostow with his now famous 'take-off', but as in a general way had been known all along, development is not a continuous but a discontinuous process. So is underdevelopment, although conventional wisdom of course denies that except in so far as it emphasizes, that underdevelopment, to again use Leibenstein's term, is a 'trapped' state from which a jump is necessary to begin developing.

Since development is discontinuous, that is, since there are *critical* periods in the development process, the same 'absolute' contribution may be unimportant for development in one period but absolutely critical for development in another. This is all the more so as the relevance of a contribution to development is not so much a function of its contribution to income but of its contribution to investible surplus. It is therefore quite possible, indeed quite likely, that even an absolutely quite small amount of capital or knowledge or something, which represents only a small share of the recipient's total capital or knowledge or something and which may not even significantly change the amount of the recipient's surplus, will make a quite critical contribution to the recipient's development if it comes at the critical time. A small marginal increase of investible surplus at the right time may be enough to permit —and its absence to prohibit— the take-off out of the equilibrium trap.

Two further observations: If Gunnar Myrdal is right, as he argues in the *American Dilemma* and in *Economic Theory and Underdeveloped*

* Nature does not take sudden leaps.

Countries, that the social processes we are concerned with are cumulatively circular, then any small contribution of capital to a developing society will, cumulated with other sources of investible capital, help to keep the process moving. Secondly, the equilibrium trap is strongest, we may presume, at the lowest level of development, that is, at the beginning. If development after that becomes increasingly exponential, a smaller and smaller share of the total, surplus (though conceivably a larger absolute amount) of capital needs to be contributed to have a given effect as the growth curve becomes steeper. The process may become, with respect to the recipient unit, entirely self propelling, a question we shall have to examine later.

What is clear is that the colonial spoilation which was part of the early expansion of the mercantilist system may have made a critically important contribution to the development of its capitalist successor's now developed members. Eric Williams argues quite persuasively, I think, in his *Capitalism and Slavery* (1944) that the slave trade of the 16th and 17th centuries made a critical contribution to the accumulation of commercial capital in Europe and—as we will see this to be significant in the discussion of the fourth consideration below—concentrated it into a few hands. Still, as Simonsen (1962) notes, even philosophers (e.g. Voltaire) had shares in the slave trade —even modern philosophy developed with the contribution of the slave, as did Aristotle's! And at a still earlier time, the primary accumulation of capital necessary for later launching the slave trade was earned by trading on religion in the Crusades. Later, Williams (1944: p. 68) notes:

what the building of ships for the transport of slaves did for eighteenth century Liverpool, the manufacture of cotton goods for the purchase of slaves did for eighteenth century Manchester. The first stimulus for the growth of cotton came from the African and West Indian markets. The growth of Manchester was intimately associated with the growth of Liverpool, its outlet to the sea and the world market. The capital accumulated in Liverpool from the slave trade poured into the hinterland to fertilize the energies of Manchester; Manchester goods for Africa were taken to the coast in Liverpool slave vessels. Lancashire's foreign market meant chiefly the West Indian plantations and Africa....It was the tremendous dependence on the triangular trade that made Manchester.

Quite a few years later still the London *Times* itself was to editorialize in 1857:

> We know that for all mercantile purposes England is one of the (United) States, and that, in effect, we are partners with the Southern planters; we hold a bill of sale over his goods and chattels, his live and dead stock, and take the lion's share of the profits of slavery.... We fete Mrs. Stowe, cry over her book, and pray for an anti-slavery president..., but all this time we are clothing not only ourselves, but all the world besides, with the cotton picked and cleaned by "Uncle Tóm" and his fellow sufferers. It is our trade. It is the great staple of British industry. We are 'Mr. Legree's' agents for the manufacture and sale of his cotton crops. (Quoted by Williams (1944; p. 176).

Williams adds, 'British capitalism had destroyed West Indian slavery, but it continued to thrive on Brazilian, Cuban and American slavery.' (ibid). Again, I cannot here of course review and evaluate all the cases in which the contribution from now underdeveloped regions made a critical contribution to development elsewhere at a critical time. Nor can I discriminate which contributions came as unexpected but fortuitously well timed windfalls, such as Brazilian gold which gave Portugal another—but as it turned out still not adequate—semi-independent lease on life; and which of such contributions are not fortuitous but are more explicable results of the internal logic of the process of capitalist development. Here, I only wish to point out that this third consideration, the discontinuities of development, must be taken account of to adequately understand the process of that development and the real contribution thereto of the now underdeveloped areas.

Mutatis mutandis sacrifices play an equally significant role in the discontinuous development of underdevelopment. Indeed, they play a greater role if we wish to take into account the fact that development is desired and attempted in the societies concerned. For even a relatively small sacrifice of surplus, or worse yet of non-surplus wealth or income may, if it comes at the critical moment eliminate a society's chances of escaping underdevelopment and achieving development for ever or for an indefinitely long time. Again, a catalogue or an analysis of this problem is not possible at the moment. But we may recall how in the case of Chile, for instance, the 1857 Depression and the War of the Pacific—both of which, it cannot be denied, had their roots in the expansion of the world capitalist system—came at a time when her economy was still budding but not yet blooming and thereby nipped her development in the bud. What if Balmaceda* had been allowed to proceed with his national industrialization programme based on national natural resources? We will never know of course, except by reference to countries like Australia and Canada who also began to do so at more or less that time, whereas the metropolitan developing power frustrated that attempt at Chile's development. True, Britain did it with the co-operation of local interests who were also opposed to Chile's progress. But the existence and power of these interests itself was only the result of Chile's preceding colonial capitalist experience. That the same continues to be the case in much of the world in our own day will appear—if it is not obvious—at a later stage of the discussion. The historical evidence is precisely that capitalism has not exploited indiscriminately. No, when the opportunity was ripe in a now underdeveloped country and the time was auspicious for development elsewhere, the resources of that country were effectively exploited for the benefit of metropolitan development. Once that mine was exhausted or the world market for its product has permanently or temporarily disappeared, the capitalists quietly folded their tents so that they might set them up again wherever in this new phase of 'development'—but also of underdevelopment—opportunity called. Whether or not the operation made a critical contribution to development, it very well may have made a critical contribution to underdevelopment.

Capitalist development and underdevelopment are not only temporarily but also systematically discontinuous. To understand the significance and importance of a particular sacrifice and contribution of an underdeveloped sector it is not always the whole of a recipient economic system but often a particular part thereof that should be examined. At a time when most of Europe was still feudal, the significance of a contribution from elsewhere was not to 'Europe' but to capital accumulation in its mercantile sector or even a particular part thereof. The contribution of profits in a certain underdeveloped country or even in all of them combined may not be directly to the American economy as a whole. They may be to a particular sector thereof, that is to the most monopolized sector. It is not so much the 'American economy' which does business in Brazil or Latin America,

* Chilean President who committed suicide in 1891 in face of reactionary and imperialist counter-revolution.

for instance, as it is a few companies, all of them big, all of them with a very significant share of the market in their industry at home. (Magdoff, 1969). It is particularly the fact that these corporations are monopolists or oligopolists at home which suggests that they have excess capacity and which suggests in turn that for them their foreign activities are quite important. To them their foreign earnings make quite a contribution, whatever the contribution to the American economy as a whole may be. Still, even this does not mean that this foreign activity is not important for the American economy, though it is more doubtful that in this respect at least it is so much of a contribution to *general* American welfare: for in supporting in a significant way the earnings of American monopoly, the foreign empire of American business may be supporting in a significant way the monopoly structure of the American economy. A more obvious instance of structural discontinuity is perhaps the contribution that foreign suppliers or buyers make to particular strategic industries, such as, above all, petroleum.

Structural discontinuities, such as strategic sectors, also play critical roles in underdevelopment. It is no wonder that in our days every country that seriously wants to escape underdevelopment is trying to get an independent, and if possible its own, source of petroleum. And it is perhaps not totally accidental that it is precisely the extraction and distribution of petroleum in underdeveloped countries that is most tightly and to them most injuriously controlled by the metropolitan monopoly. But petroleum is only an example. It is the principle of metropolitan control over the existence or in-existence of critical or key sectors in underdeveloped economies in general which may suffice to keep that economy underdeveloped. The nature of these sectors may change with time and circumstance, such as from salitre to copper in Chile, but the metropolitan control remains the same. Possibly the most critical sector for most under-developed countries over the longest periods of their history is that of foreign trade. And that is precisely the sector most under foreign control. Moreover, not only discontinuities and critical or key sectors of the economic structure but also those of the political and social structure are often relevant (insofar as it is at all legitimate to distinguish between these structures). Thus control not over all the population, but over the bourgeoisie or even over part of it and its instruments of power may be enough to keep a country underdeveloped indefinitely and to aggravate its underdevelopment over time. And the bourgeoisies are indeed highly dependent on metropolitan power.

The question of latent structure or pattern maintenance is best left for explicit and implicit clarification through the discussion of some systematic features of development and underdevelopment under capitalism to follow.

2

On the History and Sociology of Underdevelopment

HOW SHOULD WE EXPLAIN underdevelopment and the process of its growth or decline? A few recent writers give some directions, though I should add that their guiding hand is not altogether steady or unerring. But then they are pioneers, at least among our contemporaries. Their titles, especially their chapter titles, indicate the direction of their thought (Paul Baran 'On the Roots of Backwardness' in his *Political Economy of Growth* (1957); Yves Lacoste on 'The Original Causes of Underdevelopment' in *Les Pays Sous-Développés*; Celso Furtado's 'Elements of a Theory of Underdevelopment— Underdeveloped Structures' in *Desenvolvimento y Subdesenvolvimento* (1961); John Strachey on 'Empire' in *The End of Empire* (1959). I shall follow their lead but, I hope, go beyond them.

The features or marks, I should prefer to say symptoms, of underdevelopment have in recent years come to be quite widely known and agreed upon. The many publications of the United Nations and its Specialized Agencies have called them to world-wide attention. A good summary of them is available for instance in the *Tiers-Monde* number on underdevelopment and development (Balandiers 1956) or in the chapter on 'The constituent characteristics of Underdevelopment' in Yves Lacoste's *Les Pays Sous-Développés*. In a later chapter this author also classifies 'Types of Underdeveloped Countries'. I do not wish to review these features here. I mention them only to note that, despite the diversity of cultural and social forms, and of historical experiences among underdeveloped countries, there is much common agreement that they have very many common and characteristic features of underdevelopment. I submit that this is not an accident. Now a widely used scientific method of trying to account for common phenomena is to look for common causes. A widely used, though admittedly not exhaustive, method of inquiring in turn into (common) causes is to inquire into (common) history. Of course, History teaches us anything only if 'facts' are interpreted. Still, we may suitably and profitably inquire to see if there is any common historical experience among differing underdeveloped countries, and, if any, what these might be.

Anatomy and Physiology of Underdevelopment

Though it may be predicting if not prejudging our results a little, we may conveniently begin our inquiry with a historical experience which all, or certainly almost all, of today's underdeveloped areas have in common: their incorporation into and subsequent participation in the worldwide expansion of the mercantilist and/or capitalist system. This procedure does not imply that today's underdeveloped areas did not have an important prior history and continuing differences in subsequent experience as well. Nor is it meant necessarily to deny the importance of more specific parts of their experience with mercantilism and capitalism such as the spread or penetration of market organization for instance in 'primitive' societies which Karl Polyanyi stressed in his Great Transformation and Trade and Markets in the Early Empires.

We may begin anywhere and note that the spread of mercantilism and capitalism everywhere very seriously modified or even broke up, and in some cases entirely eliminated, the form of social (including of course economic, political, etc.) organization existing in the affected area or among the affected people during the period of initial contact. No less than in contemporary underdevelopment, traditional or initial 'pre-contact' social forms were not fixed but also in the process of change at the time of their contact with mercantilism or capitalism. It is therefore really more accurate to say that this 'contact' channelled the historical process of change of the various social forms into developing in a direction and way other than that which they would otherwise have pursued in the absence of contact.

The case of India, for instance, is relatively well documented. In writing his The End of Empire, John Strachey has recently again reviewed and summarized 'How an Empire is Constructed' (chap. I) and 'What Happened in India' (chap. III).

Marx had already noted the systematic destruction of the Indian textile industry in his 'British Rule in India', though not unlike my contemporaries he thought that the diffusion of British influence there would eventually result in the economic development of India. (Marx: *On Colonialism*). Recently retabulated and evaluated national income estimates for India over a 150-year period of participation in the Imperial, that is first mercantilist and then capitalist system, shows that Indian per capita income declined. Marx may be partially pardoned because he had 100 years' less hindsight than our contemporaries who, in addition to just casual observation of India's lamentable current—and I submit still aggravating—underdevelopment, have also available to them the classic study on the subject in R. Palme Dutt's *India Today* and his other works.

For an understanding of the causes of underdevelopment it is not so much the decline in Indian income or even the terrible drain of the economy that are most important, since these are in part the symptoms of the disease of underdevelopment although of course, any such weakening of the economic body also reduces its recuperative powers and moreover reduces its 'natural' defences against still other threats to its economic health.

More interesting is the anatomy and physiology of underdevelopment. Marx already noted the destruction of the textile industry, which might be likened to the disappearance of handloom weaving in Europe in response to the powerloom. But as Strachey (1959; p. 59) observes, 'the Indian case was very much worse. The English manual weavers were reabsorbed fairly rapidly....But in India... the creation of mechanized industry was delayed for many decades'. But not only the textile industry, but virtually the entire Indian handicrafts industry was severely crippled if not totally destroyed. Since handicrafts were spread through all the villages, this severely and unfavourably affected all of rural society and its structure. It affected agriculture. But the organization of agricultural production had already been severely maimed by the coming of the British in other ways, such as its commercialization for the benefit of the British and their Indian allies, and to the detriment of the producers. The first widespread famine swept the country only a very few years after British arrival. Strachey notes a highly important aspect of the matter when he observes that 'a colonial country is almost inevitably subject to these terrible deformations of its development. Since this development comes to it from abroad and is imposed on it by foreign governors over whom its people don't even have any indirect power, it is exposed to suffering the horrors of the industrial revolution, while it harvests its fruits only slowly and sparsely' or, I might add, for the bulk of its people, not at all.

Historians, particularly Marxist ones (Sen, 1962 for instance) sometimes suggest that India, and in their due time other Asian societies, had been at the point of evolving from their particular brand of feudalism to capitalism at more or less the time of contact. This leads then to the thought provoking inference that, paradoxically, capitalism extended feudalism in these societies by keeping them in the dark ages for a few more centuries than would otherwise have been the case. This interpretation rests on the additional premise that India, Burma, or as the case may be Latin America is, or until recently was, feudal at least in substantial part. But this is, I think, severely challenged precisely by the deep and thoroughgoing restructuring of Indian and other societies, which capitalism, and most especially the society's participation in the world-wide commercial and now industrial/commercial system, has produced. Since the network of social relations has been changed by capitalism, all particular social relationships, whatever their form, have become at least indirectly affected and determined by the capitalist system. The question is argued at length, with respect to Brazil, in Frank 1963 (now 1967, 1969) and we may return to it in the concluding section of this essay, which will deal with the theoretical implications of our observations.

Let us turn to some other peoples. China's productive organization and capacity was also substantially affected—and worsened— during even its relatively brief 'semi-colonial' experience with the advance of capitalism prior to her occupation by Japan. Owen Lattimore (1960) reviewed 'The Industrial Impact on China, 1800-1950', and he notes the same kind of transformation of previously viable social organizational forms into less or unviable ones, though of course to a lesser degree than we have already observed in India. In this case, 'industrial' of cour se means 'capitalist'. The well known political fate of Owen Lattimore in the United States is perhaps not so surprising when we consider that he challenges the conventional wisdom so far as to suggest that capitalism actually damaged China's or anybody else's social and economic development.

Without trying to catalogue all cases of underdevelopment, let us briefly look at Africa. African history did not begin when the white man arrived in the nineteenth century. We should recall that numerous white men already visited the ports of Africa two hundred years earlier all through the seventeenth century. And African history stretches back quite a few millennia beyond that, even if it is being again written, unfortunately, beginning only very recently—beginning essentially and not unaccidentally, with Africa's renewed political independence. And during that history or histories among others, Africa witnessed the growth and decline of such empires as that of Mali, Ghana, and Benin which produced such magnificent ironworking technology and aesthetic as that of Benin while many people elsewhere were little more than scratching with stones. Where, we may ask, is Africa's 'initial' and 'traditional' social and cultural form(s)? Leachy recently unearthed bones in East Africa whose age of over a million years easily quintuples those of European Neanderthal and doubles those of the Chinese Peking man.

More relevant, may be, the slave trade and the mercantilist sponsored slave wars very seriously modified the social organization, productive capacity, and cultural level of many parts of Africa. Little is known maybe of the specific consequences of this incorporation of African societies into the expanding European based mercantilist system, and information may be sparse also about the living conditions under already previously existing intertribal warfare and slavery. But who will argue that mercantilism increased the viability of African social organization? Or that it did not affect it but left it 'initial' and 'traditional'? Or that, transported to the New World, mercantilism there reassembled the (surviving) Africans in more developed—less underdeveloped—economic, social, or cultural forms?

The more 'classically' colonial, that is capitalist, history of Africa has been summarized by Jack Woddis in his *The Roots of Revolt* (1960). It should not be necessary here to review the implantation of the features—more important, of the structure—of underdevelopment such as that summarized for East and South Africa by the African saying 'in the beginning the white man had the Bible and we had the land; now we have the Bible and he has the land'; or the imposition in the same areas of taxes payable in money where the monopolization of land was not enough to force the inhabitants into the migratory—and socially, culturally, and productively disorganizing

—employment of labour in capitalist mines and elsewhere; or the implantation of crop export economies with their attendant economically destabilizing fluctuations but politically stabilizing (that is conserving) comprador bourgeoisies; or the politically and morally corrupting 'indirect rule', and hosts of others, not to mention the renewed or rather continued sponsorship of internecine and other warfare as in Algeria, the Congo and elsewhere. And for those social scientists who are really interested in bringing their social psychology to bear on the study of the personality and culture of underdevelopment, they might do well to listen to Seku Touré, the President of Guinéa; or if they can't get there, in the meantime to read Franz Fanon's (1962) pathbreaking *The Wretched of the Earth*. If they were any kind of scientists at all, they would then soon find out that the terrible depersonalizing colonial mentality of the colonized is not an initial or traditional trait at all, but that it certainly is a product of these people's participation in the capitalist system and a critical contribution to the development of underdevelopment. Analogous is the highly important and successful efforts of the Black Muslims to regain their personal dignity and communal ability to challenge underdevelopment in the United States (written in 1963 long before black power). I do not mean to imply, of course, that this capitalist-development-produced underdeveloped mentality is limited to Negroes. Unfortunately, it is found all over.

Turning to Latin America, we find probably the most complete destruction of previously viable social systems, at least of large scale ones. After The Conquests by Cortez and Pisarro, the indigenous populations immediately declined by half— which inevitably seriously decreased the viability of their social system and exposed it to increasing underdevelopment. The initial incorporation of these existing societies into the expanding mercantilist one was pure conquest through military (though not necessarily cultural) superiority followed by *Raubwirtschaft* which simply pillaged the already existing wealth that the previously evidently viable social systems had produced. Can there be any question but that the contemporary Aztec, Mayan, and Inca descendants (in the doubtful event that this is a culturally meaningful term) of the pre-Conquest peoples live at a lower economic and cultural level today than their ancestors did? In Inca times a letter took three days to reach Cuzco from La Paz. Today, thanks to the airplane, it takes three weeks, if it gets there at all and if there is anybody to write and read it. In Inca times, fresh ocean fish was available in Cuzco at 10,000 feet altitude. Today its inhabitants nearly starve. Moreover, their calorie intake is decreasing.

Latin America offers a still more instructive laboratory for the historical analysis of how underdevelopment developed—and still develops under mercantilism and capitalism, because the New World offers numerous examples in North America, the Antilles, and especially in Brazil, Venezuela, and Argentina of how under-developed societies which were not incorporated into, but which were virtually begun from scratch and (under)-developed by, the development of the single world-wide mercantilist and capitalist system. Since these areas had no existing wealth that could be carried away, the commercial and productive system, which in the formerly high-civilization areas developed only after the 'initially' existing stock of wealth had been exhausted, was here implanted from the very beginning.

Historians of Latin America have been debating how the conti-nent came to be colonized. The conventional view has it that feudal Spain and Portugal transplanted their feudal institutions into the New World. The apparently minority interpretation of the Argentinian Sergio Bagú (now also Vitale), is that Spain and especi-ally Portugal already displayed strong mercantilist sectors and that in their expansion and consolidation these mercantilist forces colo-nized the New World. I think we must agree with the second of these interpretations and go on to pursue its far reaching implications. Whatever its strength or weakness, a feudal system, in the nature of the case, (would have) generated neither the interest nor the capa-city to conquer and colonize another world. This fact does not detract from the possibility that some feudal lords, or their non-oldest sons, might have tried, with varying degrees of success, to re-establish abroad the feudal style of life they were losing at home. But they would not have reached the New World other than as conscious or unconscious agents of the expansion of mercantilism from Europe to the other continents. The social consequences of their activity there were to make Latin America a mercantilist and then a capitalist colony, whatever their private intentions or the local social forms they brought along may have been.

Mercantilist expansion abroad was intimately related to, above

all, the crown and the consolidation of the national state and its power at home. Whether 'trade followed the flag' after the initiative and force of the Portuguese crown or whether 'the flag followed the trade' as it did after the Dutch and British East India Companies, the flag and trade really went hand in hand. The word 'trade' of course is misleading. At the beginning of mercantilist and capitalist expansion, nobody distinguished between conquest, trade, and robbery. All were for the good of the metropolitan 'mother' country. I am not so sure that they are distinguishable in our contemporary capitalist world. Nor have the intimate ties forged in the 16th and 17th centuries between the metropolitan state and its commercial and later also industrial bourgeoisie ever been severed again, all of Adam Smith's liberal innovations notwithstanding.

In the South of the United States, in the West Indies, and in Brazil especially, but to lesser extents elsewhere on the continent as well, this European expansion implanted slavery in unmistakable form. It was not pre-feudal slavery (in the Marxist sense), nor was it feudal slavery. It was, as Eric Williams (1944) has so effectively argued in his *Capitalism and Slavery*, capitalist slavery—unless someone wishes to argue that it would add anything to our understanding of the development of underdevelopment, and to that of development, to say that it was 'mercantile(ist) slavery'. It extracted immense riches from Africa where the slaves came from, from America where the slave-produced goods came from, and from the slave trade itself, all of which, while serving as an undoubtedly important source of the (primitive) accumulation of capital in the metropole, not only decapitalized the populations of the peripheral countries but implanted the social, economic, political, and cultural structure of underdevelopment among them. Elsewhere in Latin America the predominant social and productive organization was not technically mercantile capitalist slavery, though it existed where and when convenient and possible, but mercantile capitalism combined with a whole variety of other forms of servitude.

Throughout Latin America, whatever the previous or new forms of domestic social organization, it is important to remember that they were turned to the metropolitan outside, produced for the outside and were controlled by the outside. This external force inevitably formed or transformed the entire network or structure of domestic social relations, however, 'feudal' and closed they may super-

ficially appear. But from another and I think more realistic perspective they were not controlled from the outside but from the inside,
that is from the inside of the metropole. They had become incorporated into the world-wide mercantile system whose 'peripheral',
'outside', though not unimportant appendages they were—and still
are. All attempts to examine and understand the domestic social
relations and the culture of these peoples now spread through all the
continents, must seriously go astray if it does not come to terms with
this fundamental fact—I should say relation—of their participation
in the world then mercantilist now capitalist system.

The 'independence' of Latin America 150 years ago, Africans
and students of Africa might take note, did not change any of the
essentials. It ushered in a period of 'neo-colonialism', to use a word
out of our contemporary lexicon, but which is more usually reserved
for reference to the 'liberation' of recent years which followed the
nineteenth century colonialist or imperialist wave. This is not to
say nothing changed. But independence, like several other political,
economic, and social changes of the nineteenth century were rather
more the effects of other, more fundamental, transformations than
they were themselves causes. The growing influence of Latin American economic, primarily commercial (in 1969 I would say export
productive rather than commercial), interests; the growing interests
of the nascent industrialization of England and of the United States;
the not unrelated decline in the power of Spanish and Portuguese
interests; as well as the pressure of Napoleon's continental system, all
combined to result in the independence of Latin America—and, to
use another term out of a later lexicon, led to the continent's 'balk-
anization' into separate if not so independent states; maybe, to serve
ourselves of a still more modern lexicon, we might call it the 'Afri-
canization' of Latin America.

Other changes occurred. The Spanish Crown had extended its
'protection' to the Indians, not unlike that of the British Crown
today (before the Independence of Rhodesia) to its subjects in Central
Africa, so that they might serve as a counterweight to rival Latin
American commercial interests. The British, whose industrial superiority at precisely that time made this kind of 'ally' against Latin
American interests dispensable, did not afford them any such
protection: their local overlords proceeded to exploit the Indians and
Mestizos more than they had been in centuries, robbing them in

particular of most of their land. The increasingly powerful British industrial interests also pushed through the abandonment of slavery and monopoly in their own colonies. They no longer needed them. Burn (1937: p. 52) writes, 'judged by the standards of economic imperialism, the British West India colonies, a considerable success about 1750, were a failure eighty years later'. Williams (1944: pp. 132-3) notes that 'as far as the British capitalist was concerned, no special legislation was required to make the West Indian sugar planter buy goods which the whole world was buying because they were cheapest and best.... Of what use, then, asked Manchester in wrath was the system of monopoly to the British manufacturer?.... the British West Indies in 1832 were, socially, an inferno; they were, economically, what was much worse, an anachronism'. In our words, the structure of underdevelopment had been produced among these people while they were useful; now that their usefulness had ceased or changed in form, that structure was left to become 'traditional'— or is it 'initial'?

On Diffusion of Liberalism

Without attempting a complete history of the continued development of underdevelopment in Latin America in the post 'independence' period, we may perhaps serve ourselves of orthodox diffusion theory to get an idea of what happened. Through its sometimes high, sometimes lower, pressure 'demonstration effects', the metropole did 'diffuse' its several varieties of 'liberalism' down to Latin America. We can distinguish an economic liberalism, a political liberalism, a social liberalism, and maybe ultimately a cultural liberalism and even a technological liberalism. Much of our understanding of underdevelopment then depends on our understanding of what 'liberalism' really is and of the differing roles it played in the development of development and the development of underdevelopment.

The real nature and effects of 'economic liberalism' in the underdeveloped countries, whatever they may have been in Great Britain, were already discussed by Pombal with respect to Portugal, who wrote 20 years before Adam Smith 'invented' liberalism (of course, Smith in his day, as Marshall in more or less ours, largely catalogued already existing trends rather than inventing new ones). In the

underdeveloping countries, economic liberalism really meant mercantile monopoly which made local—today we call it national—
enterprise really quite un-free to start or 'competed' it out of existence
where it had already begun. Where it served the metropolitan
economic needs and interests, under liberalism no less than under
mercantilism, *extractive* industries were set up, bought up, or just
plain stolen in the form of mines, plantations, and of railroads whose
localization quite evidently, and intentionally, prepared them to
extract towards the metropole the resources of the countries in which
they were built.

I do not wish to imply that the metropole diffused its economic liberalism only as far as the ports and immediately supplying hinterland of these countries. That is the, I think erroneous, 'dual society' thesis which holds that the vast bulk of the
population remained untouched and 'traditional' or 'initial'. On
the contrary, the spread of the liberal capitalist system affected
everyone, 'known' to the most 'isolated' subsistence farmer. His
productive capacity and activity came to take on a sort of hour-
glass relationship to the commercial, national and international,
sector. Resources flowed—and flow—in and out of his economy in
response to the downs and ups, respectively, of the commercial
sector.

The cumulative sum of his many 'small' purchases—ask the
Japanese—play a significant role in the world commercial economy;
and his residual claimant, and, in time of his but also of the hour-glass
economy's need, his 'self-sufficient' relation to the national and
global economy, all help to stabilize that economy and prevent it
from bursting apart at the seams—to the benefit of those who occupy
a more privileged position in the global grab bag, but at the sacrifice
of himself and his 'development'. The dubious should note how
'subsistence' agriculture and life increases during national or world
recessions. There must be all kinds of documentation available on
this phenomenon. For Brazil it is described, for instance, by Caio
Prado (1960) and by myself (Frank, 1963, now 1967-69). Even in
Detroit the Michigan Employment Security Commission literally
lost 50,000 workers and their families in their revision of employment
statistics for the 1958 recession year and then found them again in
Kentucky and Tennessee to whose extended family subsistence
economy they had returned to weather the storm (Frank 1960). If

we take a slightly longer historical perspective, we will note that this phenomenon is not limited to 'business' cycles but occurs also, and maybe more importantly so, over 'commodity' cycles.

When the world market for the Brazilian Northeast's sugar (the world's original sugarbowl) disappeared, this region retrenched into a subsistence slumber from which it has had only occasional, recurrent but partial awakenings occasioned by temporary calls upon its potential resources in the form of demand for cotton (by 19th century England), slaves (by 19th century Southern Brazilian coffee expansion), sisal (by 20th century war demands) etc. Today the region has 23 million luckless inhabitants with one of the world's lowest levels of living; and it suffers from what some people prefer to call 'traditional' or 'initial' underdevelopment (for references see among others Prado 1963, Simonsen 1962, Furtado 1959). The same process of the development of underdevelopment may be observed in the gold rush to Minas Gerais and the silver rush to Potosi and their subsequent underdevelopment into ghost regions. (The fact that these particular examples occurred before the 19th century is of course quite irrelevant for present, though not for other, purposes).

Latin America, and Asia and Africa too, also imported political liberalism. Though this phenomenon has received less serious attention by social scientists than has its economic analogue, I venture to suggest that, once the matter is examined with equal attention, it will be found that the contributions of political liberalism to Latin American underdevelopment have been quite equal to those of economic liberalism. Without resorting even to what Lenin taught us in *The State and Revolution*, we might take an initial cue from University of Chicago trained Anthony Downs (1957). In his *An Economic Theory Democracy* he analyses the political process and organization in the United States as a market place for votes and influence in the same terms that neo-classical economists discuss the economic market place. Now, whatever the structure of one or the other of these markets may be in the metropole, their structure in Latin America, the political one no less than the economic, has been and remains strictly monopolistic. The same is, and in the future will be, true for Africa and South Asia. In fact, it is only, for some people, a convenient fiction to talk about a 'liberal' economic and a separate political structure. There is only one such structure really, and the key positions in it have since its beginning been occupied by the bourgeoisie, largely commercial and financial for lack of any other profitable activity (I would now, 1969, place greater emphasis on the export-production bourgeoisie). Even the famous provincial political bosses represent more the commercial than the productive interests of their clients, including land-owner clients. But of course the real power, all talk about 'feudalism' notwithstanding, is concentrated at the commercial capital centre. So far 'free elections' have served admirably to keep it there. And where this threatened to be not the case, it has been preserved by what we might call 'general elections', though admittedly the resulting famous military 'golpes' have had other partial sources as well.

The supposed independent existence of the politic-economic systems of the present twenty 'liberal' Latin American 'republics' is in fact also to some people a convenient fiction. I am not sure which symbolizes the political and economic ties of Latin America with the metropole better, the earlier more predominant 'gun-boat diplomacy' or the later more predominant 'dollar-diplomacy', 'Pan American Union', 'Good Neighbour 'Policy', Alliance for Progress', etc. In Batista's Cuba, 'negotiations' between the Cuban President and the American Ambassador symbolically and symptomatically took place at the American Embassy, not at the Presidential Palace. As an illustration simultaneously of the colonial mentality mentioned earlier and of the political colonialism under discussion here, today's (October 1963) newspaper reports that the incumbent consul general of the Dominican Republic in New York refuses to yield his Rockefeller Center (!) place to his pretending successor designated by the new Dominican military junta government and that 'he told reporters that his behaviour is legal because the government of the Junta which deposed (President) Bosch *was not recognized by the U.S.A.*' (Emphasis mine, though it should hardly be necessary). In the last century Great Britain also threatened non-recognition of Latin governments who would not do her bidding such as to abolish the slave trade.

The foregoing observations, of course, do not pretend to be an analysis of the 'liberal' political structure of underdevelopment in Latin America. That would require a more detailed examination of the fundamental triple alliance between the international metropolitan bourgeoisies, the predominantly commercial national bourgeoisies who are their junior partners in the capitalist system, and thirdly with their provincial or local clients; and it would involve a review of the continuing political juggling and shifting and warring within that alliance which notwithstanding some predictions about predominantly 'national' interest appears so far to have followed the maxim that 'le plus ça change, le plus ça reste le même'. We will have occasion to return to this topic below.

It is not illegitimate to speak of a 'social liberalism'. What I have in mind is more popularly known as 'open society' and more sociologically labelled 'social mobility'. But these terms perhaps serve to obscure the fundamental relation this form of social organization has with the economic and political ones already discussed. The diffusion, importation, and consequences of social liberalism in Latin America (or in other underdeveloped countries) has received still less critical examination than its economic and political analogous, possibly because it is at least in some of its forms perhaps a more recent arrival.

The diffusion of social liberalism, like that of economic and political liberalism, is not accidental or primarily intentional. It has its reasons or causes and I think they can in a preliminary way be said to be economic ones. The abolition of slavery, which also had its economic causes, 'liberated' the slaves in other ways in that it increased their statistical chances for social mobility. The introduction of private ownership in the previously communally held lands of formerly Spanish America, which was at once inspired by and defended in terms of economic and political liberalism, quickly led to the concentration of land in the hands of those who had the economic and political power to 'purchase' it and forced countless peasants into less intimate ties with the land or off the land altogether. These economic transformations did not immediately open all doors to mobility, of course, but probably in combination with later shifts in the demand for labour, they did increase mobility. Since I am still very unfamiliar with the immediately succeeding social situation, let me come to a more recent period.

Incipient industrialization has carried social liberalism or mobility with it. But social mobility has recently also shown substantial increases in the absence of significant industrialization. In these cases social liberalism is closely associated with the expansion of a (usually single product) primary export sector which directly supports a growing tertiary or service sector without the classical, that is metropolitan, secondary or manufacturing sector in between. These maybe typified by petroleum as in Venezuela but found throughout most of the remainder of Latin America as well. In such cases the primary sector to a smaller extent and the tertiary sector to a very much greater extent offer 'liberal' opportunities for upward mobility.

Significantly, in some cases these opportunities have been made more available to foreign immigrant ex-peasants who, much more than in the United States for instance, enter the society somewhere in the middle rungs of the social ladder, thus forcing relatively more domestic peasants to stay on the rung on which they are, but not necessarily in the same occupation. Workers and employees of the foreign corporations of the primary export product business, the employees of growing government bureaucracies, but more numerous than anything the medium, and especially small purveyors of all sorts of personal and commercial services, all have, or have access to, a place in the stratification system above the lowest rung; and all but part of the last named category have similarly elevated incomes. To a very large extent, even for those in the provinces, social and economic roles have a satellite relation with the central export industry sun. As the fortunes of this industry rise or decline, or as one export product is replaced by another, as I shall discuss below, so also do the fortunes of the incumbents of these satellite roles shift. Leaving the examination of social liberalism's consequences for underdevelopment for this later discussion, we may here only note that 'social' liberalism or mobility is really 'individual' in that some, though by no means all, members of the society find the opportunity on an individual basis to move within the existing social structure.

The diffusion of cultural liberalism goes beyond that of liberal ideology unless we should honour Donald Duck with the term 'ideology'; but maybe we can't classify him as 'culture' either. In that case I don't know what all is diffused. I also don't know if we should hold that cultural diffusion in recent times is greater than it was when Christianity and Iberian culture were implanted, on the continent. But it is undoubtedly great. Is it 'liberal'? Much of it, especially as regards economic, political, and social ideology, undoubtedly is. D. Joao VI, His Majesty of Portugal and Brazil, et al., was diffused with the new liberalism at the time of Ricardo. And the most casual observation, as well as more incisive study, readily demonstrates how disastrous it was for his contemporary subjects and their unfortunate heirs. I cannot review or analyse the entire ideological and cultural life of Latin America or the under-developed world. So let me only ask rhetorically how underdevelo-ped the underdeveloped world's ideology and culture must be that the developed world's view of underdevelopment has wide-spread acceptance in the underdeveloped world itself. I should say, perhaps, 'has gained acceptance' lest some of my 'developed' readers think that I mean to suggest this self-conception in the underdeveloped world is 'initial' or 'traditional'. Sociologists take note: according to the faculty of the UNESCO sponsored Latin American School of Sociology in Chile (FLACSO) the *summum bonum* for their Latin American students is to publish in the *American Sociological Review* (under the 1963 director). Publish what? The 'developed' view of underdevelopment.

But cultural liberalism is not just 'liberal' culture. It is the liberal production, diffusion, and consumption in the name of 'liberalism' of any item that can by the most liberal interpretation be called culture or truth—such as Donald Duck or Associated Press and United States Information Service news releases. Of course, this liberal diffusion occurs not in the name of political and cultural liberalism alone. No, it is also for the sake of economic liberalism: it pays. Latin American news stands are swamped with ducks, detectives, and dancing girls which pay handsome royalties in foreign exchange to their creators and adequate payoffs to their local distributors. And when the market is not receptive enough to receive all the diffusion of the RIGHT news and views, there is always the liberal subsidy by the foreign corporations, by the metro-politan controlled advertising agencies, and by the metropolitan governments. And that is why the influential Rio de Janeiro news-paper, *O Globo* is popularly known as *The Globe*.

Technological liberalism may be regarded as the technological aspects and consequences of economic and cultural liberalism. It is perhaps best examined when we come to the discussion of the reciprocal relation of development and underdevelopment.

The real importance of economic, political, social, and cultural liberalism(s) for underdevelopment lies in their interaction to pro-mote and maintain that underdevelopment. Without attempting a very incisive analysis, we may construct an ideal type of this process in contemporary times. The exigencies of the world market or some

monopolized sector thereof result in the relatively rapid expansion—
that is extraction—of a primary export product; petroleum in
Venezuela, copper in Chile, coffee in Brazil, bananas in lots of places.
Resources flow into that sector. Though we like to think that these
resources are a contribution of the developed countries, the bulk of
them often are national resources which are only catalized by the
foreign 'investor'. Be that as it may, this industry offers elite and
other economically, politically, and socially privileged positions
within the stratification system and can even be said to change the
stratification system to that extent. Along with this elite evolve a
very much larger number of satellite or client tertiary industry
positions ready to serve the productive and more especially the
consumption demand of that elite. A variety of governmental,
banking, and private enterprise channels serve to connect the export
sun with its tertiary moons. Those 'fortunate' enough to participate
in this development rise in economic and often in social position.

More often than not the process is accompanied by inflation
to oil the wheels and especially to fill the spaces where the wheels
don't quite fit with each other. All seems well and promises to get
better, even politically. To get the process started in the first place,
the foreign interests had to get a concession to operate from the
national interest groups (who don't necessarily represent the national
interest) mediated through the national government that represents
them. This concession is most readily obtained/granted through a
strong, unified national government. Better than anything, through
a military dictator. If the foreign needs happened to coincide in
time with the existence of such a dictator, the foreign interests take
advantage of the situation. If he should be lacking at the economically auspicious time, the general procedure has been to set him up.

But some time later, the concession has been received, business
is looking up, and as we noted above the national clients of the
export sector are progressing economically and socially. The time
has come for a 'liberal' step towards political and cultural progress.
The foreign interests and government want it because it is consistent
with their 'liberal' principles, and their national clients want it as
the natural outgrowth of their progressive economic and social
'liberalization'. The dictator is thrown out; he takes refuge in the
country of his former allies or if they turn out to be only fair-weather
friends in one of their other client countries in which the economic-

social-political cycle is currently at another stage; and a 'liberal' democratic government is set up.

Times change. The quantity of exports begins to decline. Or the quantity continues to increase but, because of a shift in the terms of trade, their earnings begin to decline. Or export earnings don't decline; they start growing at (an ever) slower rate. Disaster strikes. The recent 'development' in the tertiary sector is tied to the primary export sector. What's more, it is tied to the expansion, even the accelerating expansion, of this sector. The economic, and social progress, and their political progressiveness, of the clients was a function of the 'progress' of the export sector. No secondary, manufacturing centre was built with the export earnings which could now keep expanding of its own momentum. If any manufacturing was begun it was strictly part of the client-satellite system too. No, the rise in national income that had been noted by the national income statistician and by some men on the street—though by hardly any on the country road—had been based on expansion of the government and other bureaucracies, on the residential—usually luxury—construction, on trade and services generally, and above all on speculation. The latter extends some of the clients' lease on progress now that the clouds are forming, because all any transformation creates is opportunities for speculation. One might think that if inflation increased before because of expansion, it would disappear now because of reduced expansion or decline. Not so. The 'liberal democratic' institutions exist to permit people to pressure their government. The newly privileged ones take advantage of this right, especially the most privileged among them—not excluding the foreign ones. They want to retain the economic and social positions they have only so recently and arduously attained; and, of course, what with the demonstration effect and diffusion and all, they want to keep acquiring more. They pressure the government into giving them the means to acquire more or at least to keep what they have—money. The government issues, or supports bank credit, and inflation progresses.

The cycle comes a full circle—almost. The newly privileged clients want to continue their progress. But they want even more to avoid their retrogression above all the 'middle classes' among them. They want stability. So does the bourgeoisie. So do the foreign interests and their government(s). Everybody, who counts, wants the dictator back or rather another one as good as ol'... to take his place. Someone can always be found to take the job for a time. Recently a variation on this theme seems to have arisen. During the 'liberal democratic' phase, some progressive national interests began to threaten to expand the economy too far 'out of line' for the metropolitan interests and their 'national' allies. Quick, a coup, to nip that in the bud.

The cycle leaves its mark. It leaves a structural heritage. The cycle is not a circle. It is a spiral. Underdevelopment develops ever more. The extractive export industry has, in its phase of glory, literally extracted a part of the national riches. It has exhausted that mine, or its high grade ores, or its relatively cheaply extracted deposits. It has exhausted the soil on that land and its surrounding vegetation cover. A portion of the country's best resources have been used up. The fruits of these resources have been invested not to create alternative (much less additional productive) facilities in that country; they have been shipped abroad—for consumption in the metropole, or for investment to further develop the metropole, or for investment in another underdeveloped country, that is also used to develop the metropole. The future investment—that is development—potential of the now more underdeveloped country has been reduced.

With the export industry came its satellite moons, now transformed into white elephants, and the people who economically and socially, but thanks to cultural liberalism also culturally, learned to ride on them. A whole additional set of economic, social, political, and cultural, but unproductive baggage for the productive sector of the society to carry on its back. And they are culturally corrupted by their client experience and politically conservative. No one is more conservative—nay reactionary—than those whom economic development or underdevelopment has passed by. Most particularly if they are among the provincial 'middle classes' who were prejudiced by the shift of the economic centre of gravity to the city or to some other province. Economically, socially, politically, culturally, the underdeveloped country is more underdeveloped than ever—and less easily able to develop than before.

Although the foregoing 'ideal type' (of course only in the sociological and not in my ethical sense) is derived from contemporary underdevelopment, its essential elements can be found throughout history. They are only less well documented for the past. Although for some places like the West Indies for instance, not even that may be the case. The documentation I have seen, may be due to selectivity in my reading, has thrown more light on the economic than on the political, social, and cultural aspects of historical examples of this ideal typification of a part of the process of the development of underdevelopment. But it is safe to suggest that the sugar and mining cycles of Brazil, the cocoa cycles of Brazil, Colombia and Venezuela, the guano cycle of Peru, the salitre cycle of Chile, and others, probably exhibited substantially the same features and consequences. The same can be said, as well, of course, for other parts of the underdeveloped world.

Underdeveloping Chile

The case of Chile is instructive. In the immediate post-independence period Chile achieved spectacular domestically organized economic growth based on mining, agriculture—especially wheat for export, and its own shipping fleet. It became virtually South America's strongest country. As a symptom, Pinto (1958: p. 16) notes that in 1842-3 Chile's 6% bonds were quoted on the London exchange at 93 to 105, while those of Brazil fetched 64, of Argentina 20, and of Peru 0. Though Chile's President Manuel Montt sought between 1850 and 1860 to consolidate Chile's growth principally by constructing a wide ranging railroad network (and for it being attacked by the vested interests and ridiculed as a dreamer by their cultured clients), her young economy was still susceptible to external shock. The world depression of 1857 and the later War of the Pacific set Chile's economy back seriously.

Still, the War brought Chile the rich salitre lands that had formerly belonged to vanquished Peru. Potentially a great resource on which to base a renewed attempt at development, salitre proved in the long run to be the undoing of Chile's development and to seal her underdevelopment to this day. The salitre mines had already been worked by Chilean and Peruvian capital before the War. Now Chilean capital very much expanded the production of the fertilizer which was to contribute to the improvement of European agriculture of that period. In 1878, Peruvian-Chilean capital represented

67% of the total and Anglo-American capital 13% (ibid: p. 55). A very few years later a Chilean Minister was able to lament 'Unfortunately and because of a series of forces and circumstances that would take too long to report (mostly John T. North's financial shinanigans with Peruvian shares and bonds bought up for next to nothing during the War as well as, of course his government's support, I might add)* the salitre industry finds itself entirely and exclusively exploited and monopolized by foreigners. There is not a single Chilean who owns shares in the succulent Tarapacá Railroad companies (that controlled the mining as well as transport and export of the salitre) (ibid.). Let us be entirely clear: The British now owned the capital, but they had not ever contributed it.

But that was the least of it. The worst was still to come—in two stages. In 1887 Balmaceda assumed the Presidency of Chile. It took him a while to really make up his mind—or to overcome part of the political opposition—but a couple of years later he launched the full-scale domestic industrialization programme that he had already dreamed of while he was still only a Minister of State. He was part of the 'Liberal Party' wave that was sweeping the continent and produced such analogous great, bourgeois and national figures—in the Listian and contemporary sense—as Joaquim Nabuco in Brazil. He dared to tap his county's natural resources to industrialize and develop it. The fruits were not long in coming. The British salitre interests, the British fleet, and their natural allies among the Chilean landholding and commercial interests all ganged up on him in a bloody civil war and overthrew Balmaceda in the counter-revolution of 1891. Chile's renewed attempt to develop had been averted, and the new reactionary government granted the British concessions which permitted still greater Chilean de-capitalization and British profits. A few years later, the yields of the salitre mines began to decline, and some years beyond the metropole learned how to substitute salitre by chemical fertilizers. Like the Arabs in Longfellow's poem, the British folded their tents and quietly slipped away during the night—to set them up again in some other part of the world which was just then auspicious for underdevelopment.

The Chileans were left high and dry. But not entirely without 'friends'. About the time of the Counter-revolution of 1891, we may recall, James G. Blaine was setting up the Pan American Union.

*A.G.F.

The first Pan American Conference had been called in Washington in 1889. The United States lent support to Balmaceda in his attempt to maintain his position—though not necessarily his policy. The British consul in Santiago tells us why in a secret telegram sent to his government: 'In exchange for the already mentioned active assistance against the (counter-)revolutionary forces, the Government of the United States hopes that Chile will denounce its treaties with the European countries and that it will conclude a commercial treaty with the United States' (quoted in Ramircz 1958: p. 229). A British newspaperman (there can be little doubt about the liberalism of newsmen's culture then or now) adds in a letter to the Foreign Office, 'It would be a shame if Chile, which up to now has on that coast been the bulwark against the interpretation made by Blaine of the Monroe Doctrine, would get to be 'blainian' in spite of us' (ibid.). These British fears were not to be fully realized until some time later.

Chile was still not beaten down into a fully underdeveloped structure. A renewed, substantially autonomous attempt at development occurred during the 1920's with emphasis on manufacturing and—a century after that metal's earlier cycle—on copper. As a result of these and previous events Chile came to have a working class, trade unionism, and a middle class that were not at all 'traditional' for Latin America. The post World War I Chilean development came to what Pinto calls a truly Wagnerian end in the 1929 crash and its aftermath. I shall not now review the remainder of its recent history. Anibal Pinto, now economist for CEPAL (ECLA) referring to the earlier period concludes that 'Chile, evidently, as we already said, does not figure among the countries in which the liberal scheme reached its anticipated consequences in spite of the fact that here, apart from the already discussed positive elements, there were others that strictly conformed to the theoretical requirements, such a total economic liberty and political and institutional stability' (Pinto 1958: p. 70). Chile, at one time an important wheat and fertilizer exporter to the world, is today, like many other agricultural countries of Latin America, entirely dependent on the wheat imports of the American *Food for Peace*. Nor does it have even the foreign exchange it would need to buy it. Nor is it getting progressively more developed and independent over time, but rather it may be said to be getting structurally ever more underdeveloped.

It would take many pages more to repeat the same kind of story for Argentina. It will take volumes to do it for Venezuela once its petroleum bonanza, which has condemned it to the same fate as Chile's salitre only worse, runs out unless her people manage before that TOTALLY to extirpate it from the system it was born into and still participates in as 'equal' partner. For the documentation and analysis of Chile, examine especially the works with the following suggestive titles: Hernán Ramirez N., *Balmaceda y la Contrarevolución de 1891*, Aníbal Pinto S.C., *Chile, Un caso de desarrollo frustrado;* and for an interpretation of him by his contemporary likeminded Brazilian statesman, Joaquim Nabuco's *Balmaceda*.

There are other kinds of external and internal factors promoting underdevelopment as well. Some of these will be more conveniently examined in connection with my discussion, which follows, on a more theoretical level of the relation and development of economic development and underdevelopment within the world capitalist system as a whole.

3

On Capitalist Underdevelopment

THE CENTRAL THESIS of this essay may now be discussed in greater detail. My thesis is that underdevelopment as we know it today, and economic development as well, are the simultaneous and related products of the development on a world-wide scale and over a history of more than four centuries at least of a single integrated economic system: capitalism. I suggest that the experience with mercantilism and capitalism should be understood to be part not only of a single historical process, the development of capitalism, but of the development of a single, integrated system, the capitalist system, which came to attain world-wide scope. Though integrated in the sense that its far-flung parts are interrelated and in the sense that it internally generates its own transformation, the capitalist system is also wrought by contradiction. One part exploits another, though it also diffuses back some of the fruits of the economic and cultural development based on that exploitation. The exploitation and development by the one part result in and are accompanied by the development/underdevelopment in the other part. Although there results a regional concentration of development and underdevelopment, there also develop developed sectors in underdeveloped regions and underdeveloped sectors in developed regions as the products of the same process of uneven capitalist development.

The contradiction between development and underdevelopment may be associated with the contradiction between one class and another, the exploiting beneficiaries and the exploiting contributors to the process of capitalist development. The process of diffusion from the exploiting developed metropole the exploited underdeveloped periphery may be associated, in turn, with the stratification system through which the one establishes clients within the other. Though retaining the essential and fundamental exploitative and development-underdevelopment contradiction or relation which is the source of its development throughout, mercantilism, colonialism, industrial and financial capitalism and imperialism do take on a variety of different forms in the course of the system's transformation. Being integral parts of the system, exploitation and underdevelopment can be eliminated only by destruction of, or escape from, the system. Socialism has so far proved the only effective way of doing so.

This interpretation of underdevelopment and development as the related mechanisms and products of the development of the single capitalist system over the centuries raises a host of theoretical, empirical, and terminological problems. Some of these are examined in the theoretical section of this essay below under the following titles: (a) Capitalism and Feudalism — one does not universally follow the other; (b) Capitalism and Mercantilism — their unity is more important than their differences; (c) Capitalism and Colonialism/Imperialism — capitalism inevitably takes some colonial/imperial form, but the form changes with the circumstances; (d) Capitalism and Internal Colonialism—essentials of the colonial relation inevitably occur within states as well as between them; (e) Capitalism and Exploitation/Diffusion — capitalism is the systemization of an exploitative but also a reciprocal relation; (f) Capitalism and Class vs. Stratification—the exploitative relation is associated with a single two-class system which is however complicated by a multiple stratification system; (g) Capitalism and Development/Underdevelopment — the development of capitalism produces simultaneous and interrelated development and underdevelopment, and vice versa; (h) Capitalism and Socialism — socialism is the escape from the exploitation and underdevelopment made at once necessary and possible by the development of capitalism; (i) Capitalism and Liberation — escape from underdevelopment and subsequent development is no longer possible for them as part of the capitalist system, and only liberation through socialist revolution offers that possibility.

The repeated use of the word capitalism calls for an introductory explanation. When I use the term capitalism, and usually the terms feudalism, mercantilism, colonialism, imperialism, socialism, etc., I do not mean primarily to refer to capitalist, or mercantilist, or colonialist features or traits, such as market relations, proletarianization, certain kinds of trade and political organization, which may be found to exist or to be diffused independently. Nor do I wish generally to use these terms to refer to a particular collection or, even systematization of these traits as in 'German capitalism' or 'American imperialism' or 'the confrontation of Latin American capitalism, imperialism,' etc. might be regarded as identifiable and relatively self-contained constellations or systemizations of capitalist, imperialist, traits, etc. Instead, I wish to reserve the term 'capitalist' especially, but in general the remainder of the terms as well, for reference to a single world-wide economic and social system. It is understanding the emergence, development, functioning, consequences and now combatment, etc. of this single system which is our principal task. It was, in the most important senses, the task that Smith, Marx, Weber and others set themselves as well. Though it is undoubtedly important for some purposes to distinguish among differing features of a given social system or sub-system and although to do so it may be convenient at times to call one feature 'feudal' and another 'capitalist', I suggest that ultimately, and that time has long since arrived, to employ these terms with respect to particular features rather than for the system as a whole. Very much the same, I suggest, must be done with the terms 'developed' and 'underdeveloped'. Indeed, development and underdevelopment are themselves whole complexes of traits and that are, if I am correct, the inseparable interrelated consequences of a single social system: capitalism. In using these terms to refer to a, or to the, system as a whole rather than to the various features which are derived from or associated with this system, I am, I believe, using the terms in their classical sense.

Reserving the term 'capitalist' for a single world-wide system ranging back over the centuries implies of course that there is such a system and that it is not of recent, say post-industrialization, origin or that there are or now can be several capitalist systems, one in the U.S.A., one in France, another in Chile, and others in Indonesia, the Congo or Katanga, or Luxemburg. But that is also part of the thesis of this essay.

Capitalism and Feudalism

Capitalism does not succeed feudalism in the underdeveloped periphery as it did in the European metropole. Quite apart from the arguments as to whether the social systems which preceded the arrival of mercantilism or capitalism in various parts of Asia, the Near East, Africa, and Latin America were or were not 'feudal', the process of capitalist development and its replacement of or intergration with the pre-existing and also self-transforming social system evidently was quite different in the periphery than it was in the metropole, different at least in those respects that are important for economic development and underdevelopment.

The topic of capitalism and feudalism, like the others to be touched on here, has of course manifold ramifications. I want to refer only to three. In the first place, where capitalism can at all be said to have succeeded feudalism outside of Europe, it did not do so, and could not have done so, in the same way that it did in the metropole. As Strachey notes in the passage quoted earlier, the coming and development of capitalism in the now underdeveloped countries was not a domestic development as it was in Europe but the result of external imposition and control instead. The compensatory (to the extent that it was even that) development of viable institutions and forms of productive organization that occurred in the metropole did not take place in the colonial periphery. There capital was extracted from land and mine not to be reinvested in domestic commerce or industry but to be used instead for the development of the metropole. The institutions and mentality that were created to replace pre-existing feudal ones were not ones which stimulated or permitted autonomous growth but those which resulted in and still maintain and deepen dependent underdevelopment.

The process of the replacement of feudalism by capitalism in the metropole was not, and could not have been, repeated in the same way in the periphery not only because circumstances elsewhere were different but also precisely because it occurred as it did in the metropole. Not only was Marx wrong when, referring to India, he thought that contemporary industrially developed countries like England show the not yet developed ones a picture of their future state, but he and his successors, Marxist and non-Marxist, are wrong in believing that the ones can follow the path of the others out of feudalism. While Marx's mistake about the future state might be attributed to insufficiency of evidence at the time he wrote, the mistake about the similarity of paths can, I suggest, be attributed to faulty, and I might add un-Marxist, logic and analysis. For once it is known that the colonies contributed to the capital accumulation in the metropole, it should appear probable that the process of replacing feudalism by capitalism there and the sacrifices of the peasant attendant on this process in the metropole would have had to be different and even more severe, if part of the cost of the process had not been borne by the colonies. Indeed, without the latter, the transformation of the metropole in broadly similar terms would not have been possible at all. The actual pattern from which we have derived our ideal type of the transformation from feudalism to capitalism was not, therefore an independent or autonomous European development, but was in part a result precisely of the exploitation of the colonies. It could not therefore be repeated, *ceteris paribus*, in these colonies unless they too could find colonies in turn to bear part of that burden. But this is evidently not possible in a closed world, except partially through the internal colonialism to be examined below. But even that remedy only raises the same question for the internal colonies in turn. For the same path to be followed by the underdeveloped countries, the relation between metropole and colony (foreign or domestic) would have to have changed from one of exploitation to one of co-operation, a transformation which has not so far come to pass.

Secondly, it must be seriously doubted that feudalism of the European sort existed in very many other parts of the world at all. If there remains so much argument about what outside of Europe really was or was not feudalism, it may be more due to the fact that then contemporary and also later observers and analysts of the world saw the world through feudal eyes (even if their particular situations may not have been 'feudal') than because the various institutional forms throughout the world were so similar. (For summaries of the argument about feudalism outside of Europe see for instance Coulborne, 1956).

More important for the understanding of contemporary underdevelopment and its elimination is a third question, that of contemporary or recent feudalism, if any, and its relation to capitalism. It is so commonplace, one might say universal, to refer to Latin

America, the Near East, South Asia including especially India, and parts of Africa as being feudal, or as having a feudal or semi-feudal or pre-capitalist agricultural sector that it can hardly be necessary to cite any references. The issue is not one of nomenclature. I shall not wish to discuss what we call reality here or there, but how we analyse it and how, as a result of that analysis, we propose to change it.

It is the argument for feudalism which I wish to call into question. That argument, admittedly simplified since it has many variations, is something like the following. Feudalism (or according to another version the 'asiatic' mode of production) existed in this or that part or all of the underdeveloped world before mercantilism or capitalism arrived; or, in some cases, according to the argument, it was even implanted there or developed there of its own after that time. The continued existence of feudalism is signified by concentration of landownership, various conditions of servitude of the workers of that land, apparently non-economically rational use of the land by its owners, the absence of wage labour, and in general economic, social, and political institutions and relations on the land and beyond, which are not those of 'pure', 'real', 'advanced', 'industrial type' capitalism. If the writer is a Marxist, he is likely to quote Lenin to the effect that wage labour and proletarianization of the peasants is the hallmark of capitalism in agriculture. (See for instance the already referred to Sodré for Brazil and Sen 1959 for India).

Often a society or sub-society is termed feudal even if it lacks some of these features of feudalism (as for instance by Sen, 1959). The writer then observes that in fact there is a tendency toward increased wage labour and reduced tenancy as well as, in some places, a tendency toward greater productive and commercial efficiency on some, especially export crop, farms. The analyst therefore concludes that capitalism, which has already taken a hold in other sectors of the economy, is finally beginning to penetrate ever more into the feudal countryside. Marxist or not, he sees this supposed replacement of feudalism by capitalism as real progress as it had been in Europe before and as it appears to be in the other sectors of the underdeveloped economy, since after all, what industry or modernization there is to be found there has been due to this same capitalism. From this analysis follows the economic development policy: eliminate feudalism in agriculture entirely and substitute capitalist institutions and relations so that agriculture may become more productive and thereby permit both through the demand and the supply side further growth of industry. Simultaneously, everyone will attain a higher level of consumption (notwithstanding the well nigh universal experience that the 'proletarian' wage labourers have an even lower standard of living than their tenant farmer colleagues).

In general, this analysis is based on a misunderstanding of the nature of feudalism, the nature of 'pure' or 'typical' capitalism, on a terrible confusion and misuse of terms; and that, above all, it leads to quite erroneous and disastrous 'development' policy.*

Only a few observations in criticism of this particular conventional wisdom can be made here. In the first place in the beginning of the above summarized argument the terms 'feudal' and 'capitalist' and their derivatives and 'semi-feudal' and 'pre-capitalist' modifications refer not so much to forms of economic organization and much less to a particular socio-economic system as they do to various economic and social features, forms, or even motivations that can be identified in the countryside. I am pleading here that terms like 'capitalist' and 'feudal' be reserved to refer to forms of organization or better yet, as I claim there is only one capitalist system, to that particular world-wide system. Other writers need not of course follow my suit, but the trouble is that they do—when they come to the conclusions they draw from their premises. In formulating their conclusions, they, in effect, do counsel for the substitution of the feudal system by the capitalist one because that carries with it demonstrated progress and benefit. But this conclusion about the consequences of transforming the entire system cannot be legitimately derived, as many writers intend, from an argument about the substitution of particular individual features. The substitution of 'feudal' personalistic, longer term, etc., individual relations or features by 'capitalist' universalistic and more short term 'contractual' ones does not necessarily, or even usually, improve either the consumption or the production of the agricultural workers concerned. Nor does, the distribution of land into smaller individually owned plots do so. The quite common confusion in the use of these terms interchangeably for 'features' and for 'system' thus leads to quite erroneous analysis.

* For the case of Brazil, the issue is argued in greater detail in Frank 1963 (1967, 1971) and also in Prado, 1960, while Bagu (1949) argues the matter in more general and historical terms for Latin America.

But the error involved in this kind of argument is greater and more important than that. If these analysts were to argue from the nature of the system, rather than from this or that feature from the beginning—instead of arriving there with a *deus ex machina* at the end—they would find that the feudal and capitalist system is in reality quite different than what they imagine or imply it to be. Without going very much further into an analysis of the 'feudal' system or systems, it may be noted that in the nature of the case a feud is a closed system or at best one weakly linked with the outside. Now that was most decidedly not the case in the Latin American societies which in some places totally and in others in the most important respects were set up by expanding overseas mercantilism in the first place.

Though other societies did pre-exist the coming of the Europeans, they were, as I have already argued several times above, swiftly and thoroughly 'penetrated', transformed, and rendered dependent by the advancing mercantilist or capitalist system. Even where it is argued that feudalism only developed later, as when the capitalist and slave sugar economy of Brazil's Northeast receded it is historically shortsighted and fundamentally mistaken to regard that region as closed, feudal, or pre-capitalist, partly because capitalism made it what it is and partly because, as the evidence demonstrates, the region is still eminently sensitive to changes in demand which could alter, temporarily or indefinitely, the nature of its participation in the capitalist system. It is thus, erroneous, and worse highly misleading, to regard most of the settled agricultural regions of the underdeveloped world as feudal — not to speak of going to such absurd lengths as calling even the American South or part thereof 'feudal' as Goldschmidt (1963) does in an article on that region as an underdeveloped area.

More important for the understanding and elimination of underdevelopment today is the misconception about the real history and nature of capitalism which is explicit and implicit in this, as in much other, analysis. Quite evidently the 'feudalism' view of underdeveloped agriculture and society is implicit, and often explicit, in the supposition that we are dealing with 'dual' societies, one part feudal, one part capitalist, and each part independent of the other. I have already argued that this view is seriously out of keeping with reality. But these observers and analysts, self-styled Marxists no less than anti-Marxists, then compound their error by attributing only the commercial, industrial, efficient, rational, etc., sectors of the economy to capitalism. That is they assume that what is modern, developed, efficient, commercial, industrial, etc. is produced by capitalism and that 'pure' capitalism only produces that.

The thesis of this whole essay is, of course, that capitalism has produced and means not only development but underdevelopment as well, or to put it the other way around, that both 'advanced development' and 'backward underdevelopment' are equally the product and the operational meaning of capitalism. Now the reader may again wish to object that I am only trying to use words my own special way, that I am engaging in a battle of words. True, it is in one sense irrelevant whether 'capitalism' is reserved for the developed, universalistic, commercial, or better yet industrial relations and sectors of our non-socialist economies and societies, or whether, as I propose, 'capitalism' be employed for reference to both the developed and underdeveloped sectors and more preferably still be reserved for the single system which has called forth both. But we can in no wise remain indifferent to the contention that the simple extension of the (in the conventional sense) capitalist forms or even organization to the remainder of the system would result in the economic development of the system as a whole. For that is out of keeping with reality as history has so far demonstrated it to be and it is inconsistent even with Marxist theory, Marx's expectations with respect to India notwithstanding. For the system which has produced and continues to produce both development and underdevelopment, whatever we may call it, it is not by its very nature able to produce development only.

My argument with the feudalism thesis in a word comes down to this: It is not feudalism which has produced or maintains the features and consequences of much of rural underdeveloped society, however feudal seeming some of the forms may be, but it is the operation of the same forces in the same system which produced the modern developed parts. Since the latter is usually called 'capitalist' I prefer to use that term for the underdeveloped feudal effects as well. But the nomenclature is a subsidiary aspect. More important is my contention that the evidence shows, and therefore adequate theory suggests, that, our contemporary system in the underdeveloped countries, whatever we may wish to call it, has not, will not, and cannot eliminate the feudal underdevelopment by the diffusion of the 'capitalist' development. And that, right or wrong, is surely not quibbling about words.

Capitalism and Mercantilism

It may be argued that from the point of view of the development of underdevelopment, and in an important way from that of development itself, the unity between capitalism and mercantilism is more important than their differences. I say unity rather than the more usual similarity in order to emphasize two relations especially between capitalism and mercantilism that are of fundamental importance for underdevelopment and its understanding, and therefore for development as well: the historical, systemic unity between the earlier development of the mercantilist system and its later transformation into the capitalist one, and the continued preponderance of mercantile considerations in the development, structuring, and contemporary determination of underdevelopment. For the underdeveloped part of the capitalist system, relatively little of importance has changed since mercantilist times.

The analysis of the development and transformations of capitalism has traditionally been based on its manifestations in the now developed countries, not on those in the now underdeveloped countries nor on its manifestations in its developed and underdeveloped sectors taken together. I shall not here challenge the usual contentions that for the understanding of the development of development it is useful and important to make certain distinctions between the mercantilist phase and the capitalist one and among various capitalist ones as well. But for the study and understanding of the development of underdevelopment these distinctions becloud more than they clarify. Viewed from the underdeveloped part of the world, I suggest, the development of mercantilism and of capitalism must be seen as in all essentials a single continuous process which, moreover and may be surprisingly, has in all essentials the same consequences in this underdeveloped part of the world today as it did centuries ago and since.

For the underdeveloped countries mercantilism/capitalism today is very much the same as it was centuries ago. No country once it was effectively incorporated into the system and became underdeveloped has, other than by escaping from the system into socialism, ever been able again to escape from underdevelopment. Almost entirely irrespective of when a country was incorporated into the mercantilist/capitalist system, whether it was in the 16th century or in the 19th, it now has essentially the same structure of under-development. Even the time span of participation, beyond a certain minimum apparently necessary for underdeveloping a country, has not seemed to make an essential difference. However great their other differences, Indonesia, India, Iran, Guinea, Guatemala now all share a certain structure of underdevelopment.

From the point of view of underdevelopment the identification of powerful mercantile interests overseas with an increasingly powerful foreign state, both of which exploit them for all they are worth has not changed from the 16th to the 20th century. The foreign mercantile interests and their states have only become stronger. If they relied on all available political and economic sanctions and of course on military force then, they have also done so ever since and still do so today. If commercial and national rivalry with its various mercantile and belligerent forms was then only being born, it has today grown to greater maturity. If during this time there was a 'capitalist and anti-mercantilist' brief interlude of liberal free trade, that only meant that then all-powerful Britain was able to exploit others 'freely' and that Britain was also freely able to export her underdevelopment producing and consolidating liberalism. If the transformation of the system from its mercantilist to its capitalist phase accompanied the industrialization of the metropole, it did not result in the same industrialization of the underdeveloped periphery. On the contrary, the greater or lesser contribution of capital by the now underdeveloped countries to the now developed ones through their 'mercantilist' relations of the earlier period were first employed by the metropole to further that industrialization at home and then through continued and essentially unchanged mercantile relations to prevent industrialization in turn in the underdeveloped ones.

To understand underdevelopment, I suggest, it is important to realize that the underdeveloped countries are still living in what, for them, is essentially a mercantilist system (I would revise that formulation in 1969). It may be that in the metropole with the development of industry and of capitalism, the determination of productive considerations by mercantile ones gave way, to the determination of mercantile considerations by productive ones, as Marx and others suggest. The same did not happen in the underdeveloped countries. There mercantile considerations continue to predominate today as they did centuries ago. It may be that during the mercantilist phase mercantile considerations determined the mercantile relations between the metropole and the periphery and that during the capitalist period productive considerations came to determine in the metropole its mercantile relations with the periphery. But that did not change the essential fact and consequences for the underdeveloped countries of their disadvantageous mercantile relation with the metropole. Metropolitan industrialization did not alter the fact of mercantile determination of underdevelopment in the periphery in the interests of the metropole, be these interests themselves now mercantile or production determined. The changes if any in the kind of mercantile considerations which determined underdevelopment in the periphery after the industrialization of the metropole may more suitably be examined under the title of imperialism, etc., below.

The preponderance of metropolitan (or world-wide) mercantile considerations in the determination of life in the underdeveloped countries is not limited to the commerce of these countries. Quite evidently, in the underdeveloped part of the world, for the famous primary products producers and exporters, these mercantile considerations determine productive considerations in the agricultural and mining export sectors as well. And, as argued in an earlier section, these same international mercantile considerations determine much of the existence and nature of the non-export and even of the so called 'subsistence' agricultural sector. But in the underdeveloped periphery, contrary to what may be the case in the developed metropole, the same international and metropolitan mercantile considerations also determine industrial production itself.

No non-socialist underdeveloped country has so far experienced or created an independent industrial development. If it ever achieved a relatively independent dynamic of its own, it has invariably been after a very few years reincorporated into what is from the underdeveloped world's point of view, an essentially mercantilist system. If we examine what are perhaps the cases of strongest 'independent' industrialization in underdeveloped countries, those of India, Mexico, Argentina and Brazil, all of whom launched their industrialization during the war and/or depression periods when international mercantile considerations did (could?) not prohibit the same, we will note that the continued development or stagnation of their industry is now almost entirely commercially or mercantile determined. In part these considerations are domestic ones of financial monopoly, conflict with commercial interests — especially international commerce — of speculation, inflation, etc. in part these considerations reflect the foreign trade and investment position of the country. More important, in any one underdeveloped country and in all of them, all these agricultural, mining, service, financial, domestic commercial, foreign commercial, industrial considerations are intimately linked to and determined by the operation of the world-wide mercantilist/capitalist system. That is why, as we shall see below, all their mutual conflicts of interest notwithstanding, all these beneficiary interest groups, the various domestic and foreign sectors of the bourgeoisie(s), are from the point of view of the underdeveloped countries (though maybe not from that of the developed ones) more linked than they are divided by their interests. Mercantilism and of course mercantile monopoly, survives as a single world-wide system for the underdeveloped countries and continues to produce underdevelopment there now as it did in the past.

Capitalism and Colonialism/Imperialism

The capitalist system that we know has never existed without colonialism and/or imperialism, and there is no reason to believe that it ever will. Notwithstanding the acknowledged utility of comparative analysis, most of the examination by comparison of whether 'capitalism' has existed without 'imperialism' or 'imperialism' without 'capitalism' is from the point of view of the study of economic development and underdevelopment largely beside the point. Thus, reviewers of the evidence and the literature like Robert E. Guyer (1952) in his *Imperialismo, Introducción a su problemática* argue that there has been imperialism without capitalism and capitalism without imperialism and that the Marxists and others are therefore wrong. But by 'imperialism' he means an empire belonging to a certain power such as Rome, Genghis Khan, Napoleon, England, the Soviet Union. Only one of these was associated with capitalism in the usual sense. Moreover, he argues, that the Russo-Japanese War was an imperialist war between the two powers which were not, however, at any high stage of capitalism as Lenin would have had them be. At the same time, it may be noted that fully capitalist countries such as Switzerland have no empire. But this sort of comparative analysis robs 'imperialism' and 'capitalism' of practically all their meaning and for our purposes analytic content. Far from clarifying anything, it totally confuses the issue. It is of course nonsense to suggest that there can be capitalism without imperialism because Switzerland has no empire. What makes Switzerland 'capitalist' in any important sense is not this or that feature, but its participation in a system, called 'capitalist' which extends or more, it would indeed be interesting to inquire if imperialism occurred in one but not another. But only one such capitalist system exists of which Switzerland forms a part; and that capitalist system admittedly has been imperialist. Moreover, Switzerland notoriously participates in precisely the imperialist facets, if they are distinguishable at all, of that system to the extent of obtaining a substantial portion of her income from being the world's banker.

Similarly, 'imperialism' must be understood not as the empire of some particular country but essentially as a certain kind of relation between the metropole or its members and the periphery. That is the way Lenin understood the term and, that is the way Marx and Smith and probably Petty before him understood the analogous concept. And that is essentially what we must understand by 'imperialism' if we hope to understand our past, present, and future. It may thus be that in Rome and elsewhere there was a relation which we may quite analogously term 'imperialist' (though then we should probably also call these systems analogously 'mercantilist' and ask why they did not develop as the more popularly known mercantilist system did), but that does not detract from the observation that in the recent centuries imperialism and mercantilism/capitalism have gone hand in hand.

'Imperialism' in its contemporary sense is a word of relatively recent currency which was popularized by Hobson, Bukharin and Lenin. They used it to refer to certain world-wide relations of the end of the 19th and beginning of the 20th centuries, a time of colonial expansion by the industrialized or industrializing metropole. The term is still employed to refer to certain contemporary relations such as between the United States and Latin America or the Near East, which do not technically involve colonies. Indeed, it is employed to refer to the entire contemporary capitalist system. But there was empire before the last half of the 19th century (though there had been a temporary lull in colonization during British industrial ascendancy). Why refer to that as 'colonialism' or 'mercantilism', rather than as 'imperialism' as well? Part of the reason, no doubt, is the more recent currency of the word 'imperialism'. Another part is the distinction that Marx and others wanted to draw between mercantilism and capitalism and Hobson and Lenin analogously between mercantilist produced colonialism and industrial-financial capitalist produced imperialism. This may seem again to be an outline for a mere battle of words, unless we refer to the content behind them.

Following my earlier suggestion, from the point of view of the underdeveloped countries, it may be more important initially to observe the similarity and unity of capitalism and mercantilism. Analogously it may be more important for the understanding of underdevelopment to see the unity and similarity between imperialism and colonialism of all stripes than it is to analyse their differences. Though noting their differences and peculiarities, is undoubtedly important for an understanding of the functioning of the capitalist system including its underdeveloped parts, as a whole, these may better be relegated to a second analytic step. The contrary might be said if we wish to insist that the general can only be known through familiarity with its particulars.

In any case, it is not possible here to undertake a thorough analysis of either the general or the particular of colonialism and imperialism or of the transformation of the capitalist-colonialist-imperialist system at all times and places. I can only throw out some brief and certainly inadequate suggestions. A question we may perhaps keep in the back of the mind is whether it can be said, of a given colonialist-imperialist relation that it was necessary to permit capitalism to develop as it did; or if this relation was only convenient, or even inconvenient?

The development of the social institutions and the accumulation of the capital, real, financial, human, technological, etc., that was integral to economic growth in Europe took place largely outside the feudal structure of society. Accumulation and concentration of capital seem to have gone hand in hand, expanding ever wider the range over which capital was accumulated through finance, trade or conquest and not breaking up the existing structure to such a degree that it would have resulted in widespread distribution of new wealth. We already noted that this process went hand in hand also with the consolidation of national states. For many of the now underdeveloped areas this process had the familiar consequences of increasing their absorption, more often than not by force of arms, into the expanding and tightening mercantilist network. Finance, trade, conquest, pillage, colonization with national free and inden- tured labour, with indigenous labour, with imported Indian or negro slave labour, all were but more or less efficient means to the same end. And, possibly because metropolitan rivalry was too evenly matched, the maximum of monopolization was desirable to each increasingly centralized power, though not of course to its rivals. This monopoly became injurious to the interests of the colonies, not of course to their workers but to their merchants and producers, quite soon. But that was of no account to the metropolitan power which sought only to exploit its colonies, and the monopoly system was violated only insofar as one metropolitan power was unable to prevent its violation by its interested colony and another power or colony.

The principal challenge to others' colonial monopoly came from Britain. First, through its increasing commercial, military, and para-military superiority and later through its undisputed indus- trial superiority, Britain was able to break down, or help break down, the monopoly system. As was noted earlier, with her indus- trial superiority over all possible rivals, not monopoly but free trade came to be to Britain's advantage. So much so that Disraeli was able in mid-nineteenth century to call the colonies millstones around Britain's neck. They were then, but they had not been so earlier. And it was not long before they were again to be an asset. Though monopoly or free trade may have been important to the commercial interests in the Spanish and Portuguese colonies for instance, their consequences for underdevelopment — and the role of the new national oligarchies therein — was fairly indifferent and equally great.

The famous explanation by Hobson and Lenin of the resurgence of colonial monopoly in another form as the imperialism of the late 19th century, rested on industrialization, monopoly and capital export. Insofar as this explanation was correct, we may suppose that colonies were millstones (for England though not necessarily for all others) during the first half of the nineteenth century because during this period England was relatively without rivals, while during the second half of the century, capacity for rivalry arose again elsewhere in Europe. If the earlier source of monopoly had been commercial and armed capacity, the new source was more industrial — and armed — capacity. Unable fully to expand inward and thus apparently forced to expand outward if at all during any of the preceding mercantilist and capitalist phases, the system was still unable to expand inward to full 'potential' capacity and was still forced to expand outward as well.

This apparently internally determined or necessary outward expansion of the system had not been associated with external monopoly only during the period of British ascendancy. Now the external monopoly pattern seems to have returned. As Lenin attributed this outward expansion to internal recently developed industrial-financial monopoly which did not permit domestic income distribution or create an adequate market structure to absorb all the profit seeking and profit needing capital, may we not look for, and possibly find, analogous internal structural causes of the earlier mercantile outward expansion as well? If Lenin's explanation of imperialism is so highly particular only to that time and place, it could ill help us, perhaps, to understand more recent, and indeed preceding, imperialist-colonialist experience. In fact, even in the heyday of that imperialist phase a goodly share of foreign investment was placed not in one's own colonies, but in the colonial or neo-colonial world in general.

Since Lenin wrote, some have accepted his theory of imperialism in its entirety and have applied it also to contemporary events, while others have rejected it out of hand. Relatively few people have, like John Strachey, more or less seriously examined its utility for the 20th century.

During this time, say since the first World War (really still a European civil war, as has been pointed out by observers from the periphery) two sets of double or contradictory trends may be observed: Intensification of colonization on the one hand and decolonization on the other, and ever closer integration of its parts by the world capitalist-imperialist system and self-exclusion from this process through socialism. These two sets of contradictory trends have, moreover, been superimposed on each other in various ways. The fact that the second World War was more world embracing, and the third cold and/or hot one apparently even more so, is an indication of the continued expansion and intensification of imperialism.

The critics of Lenin have all noted that since World War II there occurred a world-wide process of decolonization in the form of the technical political independence for states in Asia and Africa like that which has prevailed in Latín America for 150 years. Lenin supposed that the internally generated external capitalist expansion takes the form of monopoly colonialism. But between the two wars that did in fact take place — and cause the second World War. The rise of increasingly corporate capitalist states in Germany, Italy and Japan brought with it a renewed, or rather continued but intensified, colonial expansion on their parts. It began in force, perhaps not by pure chance, during and after the world-wide capitalist depression of the 1930's. And it took the form, in Western Europe, of an attempt to colonize even the other metropolitan powers. The attempt was, because of their opposition, unsuccessful — and even then it might have been successful if the Soviet Union, turned socialist and industrialized, had not been able for that reason to offer the resistance it did. For the previously already colonialized and underdeveloped countries such as those of Eastern Europe or for the newly colonialized ones of Western Europe, this continued or new colonialism was hardly an asset to their development. Since the War, this type of monopoly-colonialist-imperialist-capitalist expansion has not been attempted again, possibly because it failed the last time, but more likely because circumstances had changed which rendered it, for the time being at least, less necessary and rewarding.

The other double or contradictory trend has been the escape and isolation of, so far, one third of the world's population, but not yet of its productive capacity, from the capitalist system on the one hand and the intensification, by various means, of imperialism in the remainder. The new developments might be called 'American style Imperialism' partly because the United States appears to have initiated it, partly because it is today its greatest source, partly because it is today 'the centre' of the capitalist-imperialist world. Such nomenclature carries with it the danger, however, that it may lead us to think that this imperialism is associated with a particular country or part of the capitalist world: it isn't. This imperialism is an expression of the entire capitalist system today. Though differing in technical detail from its forerunners, it remains, especially for the underdeveloped world, essentially the same as all previous forms of capitalism-colonialism-imperialism: the source and systematization of exploitation and underdevelopment.

The most striking characteristic of the 'new' 'American style' imperialism is its all pervasiveness and integration. In view of that, it is perhaps paradoxical that beyond the underdeveloped and socialist parts of the world it is so widely denied to exist at all. Maybe that denial of imperialism today — and it is not only denial but real inability to see it — is partly due precisely to imperialism's pervasiveness and penetration: an ocean fish does not know he is swimming in salt water. Contemporary imperialism indeed does not rest on classical colonial monopoly; its victims are 'free'. It does not take the form primarily of portfolio investment, but rather of direct investment of a relatively new form. It takes the form relatively less of raw materials extraction, though especially in petroleum that still plays an important role, and appears increasingly as the export and foreign production of a myriad of industrial, agricultural, cultural, and other commodities and services. Increasingly, however, it involves less the metropolitan production of these commodities or rendering of these services as it does the metropolitan control and exploitation of this process elsewhere.

For a preliminary and early view of this new form of imperialism we may turn to J. F. Normano who wrote already in 1931 on *The Struggle for South America*. He quotes Frederick List's century-old but still accurate analysis of American foreign policy:

'When we judge this conduct by principles, there is nothing but contradiction; but when we look at the aim of the country, there is nothing but conformity. Her aim was always and ever to raise her manufactures and commerce.' (In Normano p. 165 from List, *Appendix to the Outlines*, p. 4).

Returning to Normano himself:

'What are the results of the struggle for the South American trade for the United States? The monopolization is not accomplished (was not intended, as we shall see further), but the real success lies in the fact that the supply of raw materials for the domestic industries has been assured, and a new market for the newest mass-production industries created and brought into permanent connection. Both of the factors which Charles E. Hughes speaks of in reference to the trade with South America have come to fulfilment.' (p. 47)

We may ask, which of these trends or what combination thereof has come to predominate in our times? German and Japanese style colonialism or imperialism encountered temporary success in parts of Europe and Asia and to some extent also in Latin America and elsewhere. But since the War, patently old style colonialism has receded all over the world. Arguing, not unlike Disraeli a century before him, that this colonialism no longer paid, Strachey notes that Britain's terms of trade did not seem to have suffered as a consequence of decolonization (Strachey 1959, Chap. XII). Indeed, Britain's terms of trade show an upward trend over more or less the whole century past. By way of further supposed evidence that the era of imperialism is now past, it is often argued that in fact the whole economy of Western Europe survived and even flourished admirably during the time of decolonization, while that of the United States went on to ever greater heights without ever having had any colonies to speak of at all. But these occurrences should maybe not be explained in terms of 'the end of empire' as in terms of the other double trend we have noted.

It is perhaps difficult to estimate just what contribution the political and other pressure of the rise of socialism has made to the granting of independence to the peoples of Asia and Africa by the metropole. But, though in the metropole it is almost universally neglected — excepting implicitly by the press and politician who warn of 'red' dangers — it is undeniable that the rise of the socialist countries has provided at least part of the stimulus to the rise of the newly, or better renewedly, independent peoples. But the influence of the basis of the new imperialism should be accounted for as well.

The United States had an initial advantage in this new kind of imperialist expansion because of the earlier growth there of mass-production and because of the damages wrought to the European economic position by the two wars. After the Second World War, however, the same pattern came to be increasingly adopted by the other metropolitan powers, and especially by the two who had only so recently attempted colonial expansion, Germany and Japan. In recent times much of the American advantage has declined as

European and Japanese cartels and zaibatsu have come to rival the U.S. at its own game. We may speculate whether that will lead to a renewed effort at creating 'colonial monopoly' analogous to those of the past. Maybe the European Common Market with its African 'Associates' shoud be interpreted as being, in part, such an effort.

At the same time, the post-war years have witnessed another imperialist development which was foreshadowed already by pre-war Germany's attempted colonization and penetration of her metropolitan rivals and which in a sense Normano foretold when he noted that production is not for the local but for the world market. I refer to the significant interpenetration of the same monopoly capital among the metropolitan countries and economies themselves. The Americans, of course, followed the German lead in this imperialization of the imperium itself after the second War. Taking advantage of the Marshall Plan 'Aid' and McArthur's 'democratization' of Japan, American capital became increasingly integrated with European and Japanese capital. Notedly, this expansion of American capital was not unconnected with an advance, albeit of a different sort maybe, of the American army in the occupation of Japan and the literal occupation of its Western European allies through NATO. On the European side, first the European Coal and Steel Community and then the Common Market, and again of course NATO throughout, served as the principal institutional vehicles of this international interpenetration and integration of capital. Other instruments utilized in this penetration of imperialism, both within the metropole and in the peripheral underdeveloped countries, have been of course the 'international' financial institutions, principally the World Bank, the International Monetary Fund, and GATT. (The Americans tried in early post-war years to create another and still more embracing organ of their expansion, the International Trade Organization (ITO) but they were frustrated in that attempt because, perhaps, it put the handwriting on the wall somewhat too clearly.*

The underdeveloped countries have not been forgotten in the process of this metropolitan interpenetration of monopoly capital. *Time* magazine (25 Oct. 1963, International Edition, p. 55) provides

---

*I was introduced to international trade theory and practice as an undergraduate at Swarthmore College by Clair Wilcox, just returned from being Deputy Chief of the U.S. Mission to the stillborn ITO.

an example: the new Mount Nimba iron ore mine in Liberia. Under the title of 'World Business' and the sub-title of 'A Mountain of Riches' the magazine tells us: ' — one of the largest reserves of high-grade ore (at least 260 million tons) ever discovered. Since then 17,200 men from 21 countries have laboured and eight companies have invested $220 million.... The financial genius behind Nimba is Swedish *Financier* Marcus Wallenberg, who saw the opportunities in Liberia and knitted together half a dozen *Swedish* mining companies and *U.S.* and *German* financial interests into a complex consortium called LAMCO... President William Tubman's government gave the company *exemption* from taxes and a mining *concession until* 2023 in return for half ownership of LAMCO. A substantial junior partner in the project, along with LAMCO, is *Bethlehem Steel*, which invested $55 million and will take one-fourth of Nimba's 7.5 million ton annual output. The rest will go to *German, French and Italian steel plants*. Dozens of companies have had a hand in building the Nimba facilities. The US's Raymond International Inc.... The Netherland's Phillips... Krupp... LAMCO has had its troubles... The Swedes *unwisely promised* to train Liberians for skilled-labour and executive jobs in advance, then found.... they had no time to do any of the training. Though the company is belatedly catching up with its promise, it has ruffled feelings among Liberians. Still Liberia has compelling reasons for *not wanting to alienate LAMCO*.... Tubman, 68, had to *promise the International Monetary Fund* that Liberia would enact *fiscal reforms* in return for an IMF loan to tide the country over...' (emphasis mine). *Time* speaks eloquently for itself, though hardly for the interests of Liberians, other than the few who will be or already are, the metropole's clients. If the passages emphasized above are not enough to give a preview of how Nimba and LAMCO will further Liberia's underdevelopment in the future, we might look back to see how Firestone did it there in its African 'plantation' in the past.

This is not the place to attempt a complete review or analysis of the operation of contemporary imperialism either in the metropole or in the underdeveloped countries. I shall only add some scattered observations and raise some questions. To begin with, it seems undeniable that capitalist imperialism exists today in the underdeveloped world, even though Strachey looks for it under the chapter title, 'New Empires Instead of Old?' (Chap. XIX), and has doubts that he has found any. He does not look very hard. The near universal denial in the United States (in 1963) of the existence of imperialism today is difficult to deal with in the face of the evidence unless it is to suppose that Americans and others in the metropole can see the problem of economic development only as one of diffusion of capital, technology, institutions, etc. from the metropole to the underdeveloped countries and that they suppose that this is what the metropole is doing, and that this is 'good', and that imperialism is by definition 'bad', and that therefore there is no imperialism, only aid and trade. But it seems equally undeniable that, whatever benefits the contemporary relation between the metropole and the underdeveloped countries may hold for the latter, it is not pure gratuitous diffusion from the metropole. It is rather the economic and political expression of its own circumstances and conditions, and that this relation obstructs development and aggravates underdevelopment in a myriad of ways. Today these ways go well beyond those listed by Normano, and include the reliance on many other institutions to extract capital from the underdeveloped countries, such as the 'world market' with its ever worsening terms of trade for the underdeveloped countries, not only metropolitan but 'underdeveloped' banks and governments to extend loans, metropolitan governments and 'international institutions' to extend loans which benefit foreign interests more than local ones etc.

These loans provide the necessary leverage compelling 'underdeveloped governments' to adopt monetary, fiscal, and trade policies which further benefit the metropole but ruin the underdeveloped country concerned, as the IMF has notoriously dug the grave of Argentina, Chile, and numerous other unfortunate countries spread around the globe—in this respect Normano turned out to be wrong in suggesting that loans no longer pave the way. (The reader may refer again to Frondizi 1958, Frank 1963, Alavi 1963 and countless 'nationalist' publications in the underdeveloped countries. Since then, by 1969, the published evidence and analysis has become very much greater).

One recent imperialist development is, however, worthy of special mention: de-nationalization of industry in underdeveloped countries. Naturally, industry cannot be de-nationalized if it does not exist. But then it is notable that post-war metropolitan industrial 'investment' has not gone into the countries which had no industry to begin with. These latter, all the propaganda to the contrary notwithstanding, remain quite without it now. But, as noted earlier, the Depression and the War led some countries, notably India, Brazil, Mexico, Argentina, to undertake their own investment in industry. It is precisely to these countries—as to the metropolitan ones and Japan themselves—that metropolitan capital has found its way. Not that it came there in the sense, primarily of new investment capital resulting in new industry important for the industrialization process. On the contrary, using its relatively stronger monopoly position, concessions obtained by the monopolies or their government, local national capital, local 'earnings' and other 'business methods' foreign capital has infiltrated these national economies, increasingly buying out or buying into national companies and *existing* installations, and increasingly gaining control of key sectors of these economies.

Part of this process occurs more directly: The foreign firm or consortium, contributing as little capital as in the above way and using the same techniques, actually does set up—or with local capital organize the setting up of—new installations, but not to produce equipment important for the continued industrialization of the economy, but to produce toothpaste or a thousand other consumer goods and services,—serving the middle class market at large profits to themselves; and *then* using these earnings, insofar as they are not shipped home, to buy into existing more important productive lines, eventually to divert their development as well—all in the name of free enterprise. Along the way the underdeveloped country pays royalties for the 'secret ingredient' in the toothpaste or the coca-cola, or the foreign technical experts necessary to produce these 'industrial' commodities etc.* The local affiliate buys at high prices from its mother company at home—or if that one wishes to avoid taxes at home, from another affiliate in another hard currency country—and sells to its mother concern at low prices.

Such 'developmental' activities of course put a heavy drain on the underdeveloped country's balance of payments which suffers from the heavy export of earnings, interest, royalties and repatriation of 'original' capital by the metropolitan firms. With balance of payments difficulties come—vide *Time* above—the IMF

*Out of 791 U.S. companies operating in Brazil in 1960, 320 were engaged strictly in service and financial activities. (*Semenario*, Sept. 26, 1963, p. 3)

and its fiscal reform medicine which invariably facilitates the foreign operations still further (after all, its purpose is to smoothen 'international trade') and makes matters still worse in a vicious spiral. And to help assure that the underdeveloped country has the foreign exchange to permit these remittances and other payments, the U.S. and other metropolitan countries cheerfully grant loans of money which came from the pockets of its tax payers but go into the pockets of its corporate monopolies.

In short, political 'independence' and decolonization have not brought with them greater economic independence or accelerated economic development in Asia, Africa, and Latin America. The postwar years have been a period of ever greater incorporation of the underdeveloped economies into the world wide capitalist-imperialist system, penetrating them more deeply, tying them more firmly, and aggravating the structure of and the amount of underdevelopment still further. Metropolitan investment in, but not contribution to, the underdeveloped economies has increased, Britain's investment in India for instance has doubled since independence. An MP noted in Ghana's Parliament a couple of years ago that before independence foreigners controlled 90% of his country's trade; now, he said, they control 95%. Latin America is ever more penetrated by American and European capital, or more accurately, metropolitan control since, far from contributing capital to these underdeveloped economies, the metropole extracts it in large quantities. The terms of trade are ever less favourable to these economies; and they promise to get worse. Little wonder then, that Strachey finds that the 'end of Empire' did not worsen the position of the metropole relative to the periphery; for it has been not the end of imperialism but rather its intensification. Only the countries which have left the imperialist sphere and turned to socialism have been able to avoid imperialism's consequences of further underdevelopment.

Still, there is visible a trend which may complicate these relations within the imperialist system still further: the effects of technology. It is often hailed in the metropole as the solution to all the underdeveloped world's problems. It is supposed that the metropole develops the want-eliminating technology and then diffuses it down to the underdeveloped periphery which thus develops. But since the metropole has not so far diffused development to the periphery and since recent developments within imperialist capitalism do not project any fundamental alteration of this pattern in the foreseeable future, it may be well to look at another possible significance of technology. The classical economists supposed that development would proceed up to only a certain level where the accumulation of capital and the consequent declining rate of profit would call forth the stationary state. Their prediction has so far gone wrong for the metropole with which they were principally concerned. The reasons for their error may be summarized as two, colonialism-imperialism and technology. The classicists had been thinking of a closed economy, but the metropole opened its economy extensively through colonialism and imperialism and thus prevented, attenuated or delayed the foreseen consequences. Secondly, they opened the economy intensively through the investment of capital in technology.

Earlier we noted the contribution the now underdeveloped periphery made to this process. To put it crudely, what appears to be happening is this: The metropole used the raw materials and capital which were historically and still contemporaneously taken from the periphery, to permit or accelerate development in the metropole itself and to produce underdevelopment in the periphery. Now the metropole is increasingly investing its own and the periphery's capital in technology which substitutes for the very resources the underdeveloped periphery have—raw materials and labour. Increasingly the metropole is indeed, as its publicists claim, able to do without the periphery, or at least to do with them, but at an ever lower price reflected in the terms of trade. In other words, now that the metropole has developed on the back and shoulders of the periphery, it really does—at least in this sense—find it possible to stand alone.

Where does that leave the underdeveloped countries? At the bottom and still sinking. Was the classical analysis right or wrong? Applied on a world scale in which the periphery and the metropole are increasingly integrated, the classical analysis and prediction appears quite up to date: capital really has been substituted for labour (the metropole has transformed peripheral labour into metropolitan capital), the iron law of wages or poverty is coming to work on a global scale and with a vengeance, and the profit rate may indeed fall and threaten to produce a stationary state—with the global periphery now poorer than it was at the beginning of the process just as the British proletariat was in fact and theory within the British classical system. The classical 'realists' never suggested that the rich would then help the poor to rise up within the capitalist system—and therein Marx remained entirely classical and realist; only their neo-classical successors suggest that, though God only knows where they got that notion from.

There are two further questions about contemporary imperialism which we should consider. These relate to political problems within the metropole. One concerns the domestic 'opening' of the economy and society to eliminate the need for outward expansion and the other concerns the creation of supranational economies. Many people who accept Lenin's discussion of imperialism for the past reject it for the present and future on the grounds of supposed fundamental changes within the metropolitan society. Thus, Strachey argues that, unforeseen by Marx and others, Britain has achieved a democratization of its economy through changes in its political organization, principally the extension of the franchise. This democratization and the contributions of Keynes and Beveridge, it is argued, have enlarged the domestic market in such a way as to eliminate the need for the export of capital analysed by Lenin. Therefore, they argue the end has come not only of empire but also of imperialism. *Mutatis mutandis*, the same 'people's capitalism,' 'permanent revolution,' and 'welfare state' argument is frequently made for the United States and continental Europe.

Neither the evidence nor any available theory promise the disappearance of imperialism under capitalism as the result of the supposed 'democratization' of the metropole. To begin with, the distribution of income in England and the United States, for instance, has remained remarkably stable and unequal during the period of 'democratization'. Whatever else it may have done, this 'democratization' has not created notable domestic investment outlets or profit opportunities that might replace the external ones. Nor has it, notoriously, eliminated the underconsumption—underdevelopment—of significant sectors of the metropolitan societies, as the contemporary negro movement in the U.S. for instance dramatically demonstrates. On the contrary, the low income and unemployment problem is getting worse precisely because the metropole has so far adopted only Keynesian, that is inadequate, remedies. At the same time, monopoly concentration continues apace in alliance with state activity, and put together, the two trends result in a phenomenon quite inexplicable —and unremediable—by either classical/ neo-classical or Keynesian theory or any known combination thereof simultaneously increasing unemployment and inflation.

Beyond that, these 'democratic' societies, notoriously also, have had to resort to an ever greater military armaments economy in order to find 'domestic' outlets for capital and sources of monopoly profits. To permit this adventure the 'democratic' institutions of these societies have had to drum up a war and defence hysteria against a quite non-existent military threat not unlike, perhaps, the 'nationalist' hysteria that was fired by the same right wing and monopoly groups during the late 19th century to sell the colonialist expansion to the public of that time. But as the costs of that 19th century imperialist expansion came to rest not only on the hysteria-blinded homefolks but also on the people of the underdeveloped world, so today the remainder of the world also has to pay dearly for the contemporary capitalist-imperialist expansion through its armaments economy. The cost to the socialist countries is of course direct and obvious in that they have to reduce their rate of development in order to channel resources into defence against the capitalist threat. At the same time this reduces the resources they might devote to development elsewhere and dims the example they set to the underdeveloped world.

For the underdeveloped countries, inevitably drawn into the metropolitan produced cold-war as they are, the world-wide imperialist, economic, political, military, and cultural—ideological policy and activity lends to their own domestic conservatives the strength that they have so far needed to resist their people's attempts to escape underdevelopment by the only available door, getting out of the capitalist-imperialist system into the socialist one. All the superficial talk about bargaining, opposing blocks off against each other notwithstanding, the principal and most important effect of the metropolitan military and cold war policy for the underdeveloped countries is quite clearly the continuance and deepening of their underdevelopment. Militarism, thus, far from being a 'domestic' measure, is a global, capitalist system-wide one.

Beyond these reasons for doubting that the 'democratization' of the metropole will lead to the end of imperialism as well as of empire, it must be noted that relations among people in the world as a whole have not been similarly 'democratized'. The world forum of the

U.N. is not, after all, a state, democratic or not. The world ha
become monopoly capitalism's oyster. Even if it were the case
which it is not, that circumstances within the metropole no longer
required monopoly exploitation of the periphery, that would not be
enough to eliminate it, if it nonetheless remains profitable and if the
periphery has not found a way to avoid it.

Like many others, Normano (1931: p. 69) noted that the imperialist
expansion of the giant monopolies is always accompanied by the
good offices of their governments. As I suggested earlier, this feature,
all 'private' enterprise notwithstanding, has never disappeared
since its birth in early mercantilist times. What may seem partially
to call this aspect of capitalist economic and political organization
into question is the appearance of the aforementioned metropolitan
international economic integration and the accompanying more or
less formal political supra- or superstate forms. Up to now none of
these supra-national political institutions have assumed the form,
integration, or force to withstand the attack of the more highly
integrated state when conflicts of interest among the monopolies
leads them to use their control over their respective states to mobilize
the states themselves against each other. An analysis of the political
consequences of such intra-metropolitan rivalry is however beyond
the scope of this essay, except insofar as it affects the fortunes of
the underdeveloped world. With respect to intra-metropolitan
rivalry's effects in the periphery, it is safe to predict that short of
serious intra-metropolitan war, the underdeveloped countries are
not likely to benefit in any notable way. On the contrary, if the
Congo is any guide to the future, the periphery will have to pay
dearly for that aspect of world capitalism as well. The increased
bargaining power, if any, that supposedly accrues to the periphery as
a result of intra-metropolitan rivalry does not, of course, accrue to
the periphery's people but at best to its bourgeoisie and/or sections
thereof.

Strengthening the bourgeoisie however, in the underdeveloped
periphery due to this or any other cause can, as will be argued
below, only lead to structurally still more severe underdevelopment.
Moreover, intra-bourgeois rivalry in the metropole, or in the periphery, is not likely to go to the extent of leading in the long run to an
alliance between any part, especially metropolitan, of the bourgeoisie
and any really progressive popular force in the underdeveloped

periphery. There is not much hope for the periphery in this kind of rivalry. Should the intra-metropolitan rivalry lead to war, it is most likely to take the form, initially, of intra-periphery war such as that breaking out, as I write (1963), over the iron ore deposits along the Algerian-Moroccan border. Only if intra-metropolitan war again seriously weakens or destroys the capitalist system, is it likely to benefit the underdeveloped periphery. There is, we must remember, honour among thieves when it comes to a threat from those they rob.

To summarize this section again, history demonstrates that mercantilism, capitalism, colonialism, and imperialism are inextricably intertwined and that, however great the changes in form among them may have been or promise to be, capitalism/imperialism has never ceased to exploit the underdeveloped periphery to the benefit of the developed metropole.

Capitalism and Internal Colonialism

The colonialist-imperialist manifestations of capitalism occur not only between countries but equally so within countries. The international pattern of development-underdevelopment is reproduced on the national level between regions and economic sectors. (Discussion of the differences between the international and national patterns may be delayed until after we have looked at the more important similarities, or rather, at the unity between them). It is of course commonplace knowledge that there exist relatively more developed and relatively more underdeveloped regions and sectors within countries just as there do between them. The gap between development and underdevelopment is often greater nationally than internationally. Moreover, in general the more underdeveloped a country is as a whole, the greater its internal development-underdevelopment gap. The per capita income difference between Brazil's richest state, Guanabara, and its poorest, Piauí, is 10 to 1, or more than that between the U.S. and Brazil. More accentuated still is the difference between a 'progressive' economic sector, such as petroleum or even 'modern commercial' agriculture and other sectors such as 'backward' subsistence agriculture. These differences appear in the developed countries, such as between the North and South in the U.S. or England and Scotland in Britain, as well as in the underdeveloped ones.

Regional and sectoral development and underdevelopment cannot be adequately understood except in relation to each other, and, of course, to capitalist development on the global level. The conventional wisdom about development and underdevelopment on the national level, which regards regional development to have been achieved independently and/or by diffusion from the metropole while it supposes regional underdevelopment to be 'initial' and 'traditional' is as inadequate as the conventional wisdom's approach on the international level. Like national underdevelopment, regional underdevelopment has developed along with and as a result of regional and metropolitan development. Regional and sectoral development, in turn, has on the national level been achieved at the cost of regional underdevelopment, and probably to a degree greater even than was metropolitan development. In other words, certainly since the introduction of capitalism, the history of development and underdevelopment within countries has been one of colonialism as has that between the metropole and the periphery. Following Pablo Gonzales Casanova (1963) and C. Wright Mills, before him, we may call this 'internal colonialism'. As we have been able to identify a global metropole and periphery, we can analogously identify metropole and periphery on the national level. More important, the essentials of the metropolitan-peripheral relation and of its consequences particulary for underdevelopment are the same.

Instead of trying to catalogue or analyse internal colonialism as it has appeared in so many places in the world, it may be better to make only a few brief observations about it which contrast with the conventional take-off diffusion approach to development and underdevelopment. This may serve as a basis for the subsequent examination of the relation between international and internal colonialism and imperialism.

A typical case of internal colonialism in a developed country is the relation between North and South in the United States. In *Scientific American*'s September 1963 issue on 'Technology and Economic Development', Arthur Goldschmidt describes the American South as, until recently, a typically underdeveloped area. (Referring for the moment to the pre-WW II South). Not only does the South have a relatively lower income, but it is an agricultural raw materials producer and exporter, heavily dependent on a single crop. It was, Goldschmidt notes, described in 1937 by the Southern historian

Walter Prescott Webb in his *Divided We Stand,* as subject to 'economic imperial control of the North,' which took the form of restrictive licensing, discriminatory pricing and freight rates, investment of Southern Insurance funds in northern industry, etc. Goldschmidt also paraphrases approvingly Gunnar Myrdal's theoretical formulation of the cumulative process of circular causation, which makes the rich richer and the poor poorer. He even calls the South a 'quasi-colonial' region. One might think that he pursues his analysis more or less in the terms outlined in this essay. But he doesn't. On the contrary, he remains quite within the limits of conventional wisdom. He says that Northern and U.S. growth generally 'passed the South by'—implying that the North took off by itself and eft the South behind where it was as Asa Briggs, in his introductoiy essay to the same issue explicitly claims happened on a world level. And Goldschmidt then argues that in recent years the South has escaped from its Myrdalian vicious circles, and that the problem of its underdevelopment has been solved by diffusion from the North, albeit through federal government intervention. This argument is not supported by the evidence, however.

Goldschmidt does not tell us that the South was created as an underdeveloped region from the very beginning. It started as a British colony, and later became at once a British and a Northern one. The Northern textile industry was built with Southern cotton and Southern slaves. The perpetual tariff issue was nothing but a continual battle over a tariff which served to develop the North and to underdevelop the South. The Civil War was in this sense a typical colonial war, and it was its victory in this War which permitted the North's ultimate continental and industrial expansion and development. All the while, the South became ever more dependent and underdeveloped. The carpetbagger was the symbol and the executor of its underdevelopment.

Thanks in part to the South's participation in a 'democratic' state in Strachey's sense, it has, as Goldschmidt argues, been able in recent decades to obtain an increasing share of American investment *as a region.* But Goldschmidt's own data belie his claim that this has solved the problem of underdevelopment. 'The measures that achieved the most spectacular changes,' in producing the recent supposed economic development, he says 'were those that attacked the root problems of Southern agriculture': 'land reform' (in the broad sense used by the UN) (p. 229). This is the land reform that is so universally recommended as the palliative for economic development problems elsewhere in the world by those who, like Goldschmidt, see only relations that are physically in that region to be relevant to its underdevelopment. He tells us that 'the small uneconomic farms are disappearing,' that the number of farms has been halved and their average acreage doubled, and that the number of tenants has declined sharply. What he does not tell us is that this inevitably means very much increased effective concentration of land in the South (as is the trend elsewhere in the U.S. and the capitalist world in general) and forced expulsion of the agricultural workers from the land. What happened to the tenants and small owners? They certainly did not become medium and large landowners whose number halved or more. They are the rural exodus. They, or those they replace at the next migratory stage, are among the 5·5 million Southern migrants between 1940 and 1960 who have gone to the North and West. With their post-migration born children they may account for 10 million Southern 'poor white' and Negro residents of Northern city slums today. The problem of domestic underdevelopment and exploitation under American capitalism has not, therefore, been solved as Goldschmidt claims. It has only been shifted regionally and sectorally. The Southern bourgeoisie may be participating in American capitalism in a different style than before. The structural underdevelopment that has befallen the Negro since the beginning has not been solved, or he would not 'March on Washington'. Nor will any march on Washington solve this problem of underdevelopment—of internal colonialism. For Washington cannot solve it. It is too close to New York.

In the underdeveloped countries, internal colonialism, and the resulting underdevelopment is even more severe. Like colonialism-imperialism in general and like internal colonialism in the metropole itself, the internal colonialism that we now know in the underdeveloped world is the product of capitalism. It is capitalism itself. It is another name for the process through which the inland Northeast of Brazil became the coastal Northeast's cattle producing and supplying underdeveloped periphery while the Coast was a regional or national sugar producing metropole, which however was itself the colonialized periphery of the European metropole. It is the process and relation by which Brazil's now Southern metropole developed, and still develops, at the expense of the Northeast and the remainder of the country. To appreciate the contribution of the peripheral country to the development of the Sao Paulo metropole, the South's extraction from its hinterland of bank deposits, of foreign exchange earned by peripheral primary goods exports, of skilled and educated labour, by unfavourable terms of trade, by inflation, by commercial monopoly, by political control, and so on—all these must be evaluated in the same terms of surplus, discontinuity, etc. that were later already outlined in connection with the periphery's contribution to the world metropole (this was partly done by the author in the section on internal colonialism in Frank 1967, 1971). In countries with still less autonomous and self-sustaining regional or sectoral development, the question is even more imperative: Where did Lima's wealth come from, of Salisbury's, or Beirut's? Where is it produced, and by whom? How is it acquired and concentrated in the capital? And what are the consequences for the periphery? Underdevelopment. What those who say that Sao Paulo is the locomotive which pulls 21 cars (states) don't add is that they are the coal cars which supply the engine with her fuel.

If international metropolitan colonial exploitation produces more underdevelopment in the periphery than development in the metropole, then it is all the more so the case that the relation between the various national metropoles and their respective regional peripheries produce and maintain underdevelopment in the latter. Conventional wisdom has it that underdevelopment in the provincial periphery must be laid at the door of provincially generated and maintained economic inefficiency and low productivity, change resisting social and cultural institutions, and when political factors are admitted to have any bearing at all, of landlord held 'feudal' political power Were it not for these factors and for the fact that the national metropole's public and private administrative aparatus is relatively also too underdeveloped to permit sufficient diffusion from the metropole to the periphery, the latter would develop apace. But conventional wisdom excludes not only the internal economic colonialism already referred to but also the elementary fact that effective political power in the underdeveloped countries is not spread around the periphery but is concentrated at the centre where it is shared by the local bourgeoisie and the capitalist world metropole and their local representatives.

It is not any inadequacy or their administrative capacity but the inadequacy of their capitalist generated interests in developing the periphery which primarily causes, maintains and promotes underdevelopment in the periphery. True, there are forces in the periphery also in whose interest it is to keep it underdeveloped; and the metropolitan interests and power maintain an effective alliance with them. But this alliance exists—and persists—essentially because it is in the interest of the heavily preponderant metropolitan forces. It is they, 'nationals' and foreigners, above all, and not the bulk of the people in the periphery who are responsible for the underdevelopment. A matter to which we shall have to return below.

Looking at today's underdeveloped countries, it must be observed that, in the first place, it was more often than not international colonialism that determined what 'national' is, that is what and whom the the boundaries of the national states in the underdeveloped world include and exclude. Though many of these determinations were made in the past and often on grounds that may not be relevant today, it is not uncommon for underdeveloped states and boundaries to be reshuffled by the metropole today if it is in its interest. The creation of Malaysia is a particularly flagrant example, designed primarily to serve the interests of the British and American metropole and secondly those of some of the bourgeois groups in the area who are their clients. It is specifically and directly aimed at popular, progressive, and libertarian movements in the area which might prejudice these metropolitan and local 'national' bourgeois interests.

At times, it is not union that is indicated but rather separation as occurred, at the instance of France, between Senegal and Mali. Or boundaries are changed or threatened at the instigation of the metropole as in both the last and this century's Paraguayan wars, and many others. Or a new state is simply carved out of the territory of one or more states or peoples, as when the imperialist metropole created Israel and put it, so to speak, under U.N. protection. Or parts of states are occupied by a metropolitan power and transformed into literal puppets as in Korea, Taiwan (Formosa), Vietnam. Beyond that the multi- and sub-national 'Balkanized' and 'Africanized' states inherited from the colonialist metropole, more often than not with inadequate resources to boot, are contributing to underdevelopment—hardly to development—throughout Asia, Africa and Latin America.

Of course, these metropolitan colonialist machinations often were and are carried on with the support of the local 'national' group which is to receive a share in the advantage from the arrangement. But this kind of bribery or pay-off arrangement, far from auguring well for development of these countries, only makes the structure of their underdevelopment more secure.

It is then the linked and superimposed relations of international, national (internal), provincial, sectoral, etc. colonialism which is of the greatest importance for the understanding of development and even more of underdevelopment. We might equally well say that it is international, national, provincial, etc. capitalism that is at issue. For it is one and the same.

In the process of mercantilist and capitalist expansion and development the metropole came to establish its trading outposts throughout the periphery. This process, or rather its results, have been popularized under the 'dual society' thesis associated with Boeke (1942, 1953) and others according to which these posts are part of the metropolitan economy on peripheral soil. We must agree that this part of the thesis is substantially correct irrespective of whether it refers to outposts which were so created by the metropole from scratch or whether it deals with parts of the pre-existing peripheral economy and society which were, through capitalism's expansion, so incorporated into the world capitalist system. But this thesis goes further and claims that these metropolitan outposts are socially, economically, and politically isolated from their respective peripheral hinterlands, or that these hinterlands are isolated and independent from them—hence the reference to a 'dual society'. It is this part of the thesis that the evidence does not support. Instead, as much of the preceding discussion already demonstrates, these peripheral outposts of the world metropole are themselves metropolitan centres to their respective peripheral hinterlands. But in addition to having the same essential relation with their periphery as does the world capitalist metropole with its periphery, these regional or national metropolitan centres serve the additional function of mediating between the world metropole and the periphery. That is to say, international imperialism/colonialism is linked to this national periphery through the national metropole in a chain fashion—and international imperialism is superimposed over the various internal colonialisms.

Insofar as we can and wish to identify still another element in this chain, that of the provincial controlling elements in production and above all in commerce, they are linked together as a further extension of the chain. Each, from the world capitalist metropole to the provincial periphery, is a veritable client of the other, selling the product of his colonialist exploitation of those beyond him to those to the centre of him. In the process, we might add, he sells himself. It is important to remember that however archaic, feudal, or otherwise quaint the outlying links may seem, they are links in a strictly capitalist chain, all of them encased ultimately in the capitalist imperialist world system.

Whatever their economic, social, political, cultural functions may have been 'initially' in their 'traditional' societies, the determinant function of the world-peripheral-but-national metropolitan centres has since their incorporation into the world capitalist system become that of mediating between the metropole and the periphery. It is through them that the metropole expanded into the far corners of the globe. It is to this process and function that they owe their current prosperity and development, if any; and it is to the same process and their function of co-operating in it with the metropole, albeit as a junior partner, that the remainder of the world, accounting for by far the largest part of its population, owes its underdevelopment. The 'developed' symptoms of this capitalist structure and process are all too visible as in the ultra-modern construction on Lagos' central downtown island, or the cloverleaf super expressways in Caracas, or the airconditioned metropole is of the Near East while the Nigerian, Venezuelan, and Arab peoples become ever less able to extricate themselves from underdevelopment without breaking the structure that produces it. It might be objected that there are exceptions or amendments to this picture; that the buildings in Lagos are constructed by foreign companies; that Brazil's coffee industry was nationally financed; that Brazilian and Mexican industry work for the national market. But that does not alter the essentials significantly; it only aggravates them. The resources with which foreign firms build in Nigeria ultimately come from Nigerians, or the foreign firms would have no interest at all in so employing them there. The fact that Brazilian coffee expansion was financed by Brazilians but came to be controlled by and to yield major benefits to the capitalist world metropole is only further evidence and cause of the national metropole's collaboration, essentially forced though it may be,with the world metropole in the underdevelopment of its own countries. National industry or national and autonomous commercial and agricultural exploitation by the internal metropole of its periphery might appear to be an exception to this chain relationship between international and internal colonialism. But, as argued above, national industry is not in fact independent; and, as we shall argue below, the national bourgeoisies are also not independent or autonomous. That is the difference between national or internal colonialism and world or international colonialism or imperialism.

Capitalism and Exploitation/Diffusion

The history of capitalist development and its theoretical treatment in received literature display the simultaneous occurrence of exploitation and diffusion. Though they may not be analytically equivalent the concepts of exploitation and diffusion can help us put some further order into the complex process of the development of development and of underdevelopment under capitalism. (This is not to suggest, of course, that exploitation and diffusion occur only under capitalism).

There has been widespread emphasis on the role of diffusion in development and underdevelopment. It is claimed that development is or will be the result largely of the diffusion of the social, economic, political, and cultural requisites of development from the developed centre(s) to the underdeveloped periphery(ies). There is and always has been reverse diffusion as well flowing to the centres of development, culture, etc. from their peripheries. Redfield (1962) for instance discussed this diffusion in opposite directions in his discussion of high and low culture within a single social or cultural area. This essay has of course, been emphasizing the diffusion from the periphery to the metropole which contributed and still contributes to the development of the latter. Though as we have noted, not all diffusion is necessarily beneficial to the recipient. Vices as well as virtues are diffused as in the case of the 'American way of life' for instance.

What may be a beneficial virtue in one place may be or become a pernicious vice in another to which it has been diffused. This has been largely the case with the diffusion of liberalism from the metropole to the now underdeveloped periphery. But there is also a stream of diffusion from the metropole to the periphery which does (potentially) contribute to the latter's development. Most of it is accounted for by technology and little of it by capital or institutional and cultural forms. If I have devoted little or no space to this development facilitating diffusion in this essay it is because it has received so much study elsewhere, while other matters discussed here have not, and because if we combine this diffusion with the remainder of the relationships between development and underdevelopment, this 'positive' diffusion has evidently not been enough to permit development in the periphery or to avoid its underdevelopment.

A third reason for not having examined this beneficial diffusion is that a particular occurrence of diffusion, or any set thereof, or even all of diffusion cannot be adequately understood and evaluated if it is examined only individually and out of the context of the entire relationship between the source and recipient of that diffusion. McKim Marriott (1952) showed dramatically how the diffusion of apparently beneficial technology hindered the productive and consumption interests of Indian villages when this diffusion was examined in the context of the recipient villages' total, even local, social system. Similarly, it is also inadequate to evaluate American wheat shipments to country X or a particular aid project in country Y outside of the context of the entire relation between the United States and that country. Although the wheat or the technical aid may make a particular contribution in a particular situation, they are usually inseparable parts of a whole network of relations between the metropole and the periphery which, as we have seen, are highly prejudicial to the latter. It is therefore important to understand the system as a whole in order to understand its parts.

It has of course long been recognized in principle, if not always in practice, that to understand the parts we must understand the whole —and vice versa. We may, in fact, interpret much of traditional social science as an attempt to examine the whole system of diffusion channels. Not only in sociology but also, and maybe especially, in economics it has been a principal analytic theme to understand the system as a whole. According to the general equilibrium system of economists and of sociologists, there is tow—or multiway diffusion throughout the system. The most conscious economic analysts of the system, such as those of the Chicago school, make a special point

of arguing that we cannot rely on evaluating a particular diffusion
here or there, and finding it unsatisfactory, take measures to alter or
rechannel it by minimum wage legislation or ceiling prices, etc. The
cure may be worse than the disease, they argue. We must evaluate
not that particular element but its place in the system or structure
as a whole. And such well intentioned alterations of the diffusion
channels are likely to interfere with the functioning of the system as
a whole by changing its structure for the worse. The principle is the
same, evaluating the part as it participates in the whole. The difference between their argument and the present one is about how the
system as a whole does in fact function.

Neo-classical economic analysis, to put it in slightly non-classical
terms, has it that the structure of the market economy results in a
tendency toward equilibrating reciprocal diffusion. International
trade theory applies the same principle to the economic relations
among countries, including what is here called the metropole and
the periphery (of course if the real world were like this model there
would be no metropolitan/periphery distinction). The Hecksher-
Ohlin theorem, specifically, has it that trade among nations will tend
to equalize factor prices among them. It does not really say that it
will tend to equalize income, to say nothing of development, among
them or that the tendency will necessarily be consummated. Nonetheless, for reasons that are not quite clear Western economists, including
among them post-Keynesians who recognize certain market imper-
fections, generally assume that the world and internal market
structure really does produce equalizing diffusion.

The evidence, both contemporary and historical, evidently belied
this diffusionist thesis. As Myrdal (1957) notes in his *Economic Theory
and Underdeveloped Regions*, that what Hirschmann calls the backwash
effects outweigh on balance the 'spread' (Myrdal) or 'trickling down'
(Hirschmann 1958) effects. In fact, as Myrdal notes and the Bible
foretells, the rich get richer and the poor get poorer. Instead of having
a general equilibrium system, we have, Myrdal says, a self-reinforc-
ing circular cumulative spiral which results in the further development of the metropole and the further underdevelopment of the
periphery. Why, we may ask?

Exploitation. Our review of historical and contemporary features
of development and underdevelopment displays not only diffusion,
spread or otherwise, but also exploitation. Marx's theory of surplus

value led to the recognition of exploitation in the capitalist organization of the productive and distributive process. If we do not accept, as we cannot, that each factor and its owners receives his 'marginal product' or contribution, then even the classical Ricardian iron law of wages demonstrated the essentially exploitative character of the capitalist development process. But the real importance, for our understanding of the problems of our concern, of exploitation is not so much that some people exploit others but that, as the historical record shows empirically and as Marx and others have demonstrated theoretically, the very structure of the capitalist system invariably produces exploitation. Capitalist structure and organization is diffusionist and exploitatory. As Marx showed theoretically and all economic historians have verified empirically, development and industrialization, even if examined within the metropole itself as has conventionally been the case, rested on exploitation and consisted of the fruits, but also the sacrifices, thereof. This essay has tried to suggest that examining the development of capitalism in the metropole and the periphery put together also shows up exploitation as the cause of development and of underdevelopment. Capitalist development has demonstrated itself to be a contradictory process, diffusionist and exploitative, based on a bourgeoisie and a proletariat, resulting in development and underdevelopment.

For the understanding of a complex reality and for the formulation of policy adequate to change it, it is essential to distil out of the myriad of particular and changing social relations the fundamental structures which give rise to them. In the case of capitalism the structure we have been able to identify is exploitative; and it inevitably produces, in reference to our present interests, development and underdevelopment. The important question for understanding and policy is not whether or not this or that particular relationship is or is not exploitatory or diffusionist. The question, as bourgeois and Marxist economists and sociologists alike have always emphasized in principle, is rather what the connection of that relationship is with others and of both with the underlying structure which they produce and which produces them. Neo-classical and Keynesian economic theory and functionalist theory in sociology and anthropology, and the balance of power theory of international relations all say that this structure is basically and essentially harmonious and equilibrating. Marxist theory and the evidence it presents suggests that the structure is contradictory and evolutionary. The former says it results in development and general welfare. The latter, if not misinterpreted, .that the structure produces development and underdevelopment, unearned benefit and unrewarded sacrifice. The ones say the system and its structure should be maintained, preserved, defended. Marxian theory properly understood and applied, calls for the system's abandonment, or destruction.

Capitalism and Class v. Stratification*

Capitalism is a two-class system combined with multiple stratification. The problems of the relation between class structure and social stratification, the exploitative structure and diffusion, the structure of development and of underdevelopment are at once among the most complicated and the least studied of the problems that face us. Literally the only contemporary treatment of this problem area that I have seen is that of Rodolfo Stavenhagen in his 'Estratificación Social y Estructura de Clases' in *Revista de Ciencias Políticas y Sociales*, in 'Las relaciones entre la estratificación social y la dinamica de clases', and in his book-length manuscript still in preparation (both now published as Stavenhagen 1969).

What sets Stavenhagen's work apart from all the rest for our purposes is that he distinguishes between class and stratification, that he seeks to understand the relations between and within them, and that he derives his analysis from an extensive and intensive examination of the social realities, past and present, of underdeveloped areas, principally in Africa and Latin America.

Before returning to Stavenhagen and the problem at hand, we may with profit turn to Talcott Parsons' lucid outline of the methodological problems involved. In his 'Social Classes and Class Conflict in the Light of Recent Sociological Theory', Parsons distinguishes the basis of Marxist analysis which he rejects as inadequate from that of 'modern' sociological theory which he recommends. Note that the

---

*The reader will note that this section is the least empirically grounded and most speculative one of all. The author has only recently been able to advance empirically derived theoretical formulations of how the colonial structure determines the class structure and the stratification system in Latin America (Frank 1970).

basis of his rejection and acceptance, in turn, is according to Parsons exactly the difference he highlights. The Marxists, he claims

> 'treat the socioeconomic structure of capitalist enterprise as a *single indivisible entity* rather than *breaking it down* analytically into a set of *distinct variables* involved in it. It is this analytical breakdown which is for present purpose the *most distinctive feature of modern sociological analysis*.... It results in a *modification of the Marxian view*...the primary structural emphasis *no longer* falls on...the theory of *exploitation* but rather on the structure of occupational roles within the system of industrial society. In that society there are "the interrelations of a series of more particular factors the combination of which may vary, therefore, conflict does not have the order of inevitability," and exactly how serious the element of conflict is becomes a matter of empirical investigation.' (*Emphasis mine*)

But the principal methodological thesis of this entire essay has been that to understand the social reality before us we must and should treat it as a single indivisible entity if that is what it is and that the analytical breakdown of this reality into distinctive variables, which Parsons quite accurately identifies as the most distinctive feature of modern sociological analysis, inhibits or prevents any adequate understanding of that reality. Parsons' analysis of the methodological essential of Marxist and 'modern' theory is entirely correct. Only his judgment about the utility and desirability of the one and its methodological procedure is quite mistaken.

Parsons quite accurately points out that when we refrain from treating the structure of capitalist enterprise (system) as a single indivisible entity but break it down then the emphasis on exploitation does not appear. Similarly, as this essay has tried to show, when we do not treat the system as a single entity, development and underdevelopment do not appear as its interrelated consequences. Instead, both may appear, as they do to conventional wisdom, as distinct, separately determined, variables (we continue to rely on Parsons' methodological analysis and terminology). And as Parsons further notes, if we treat the capitalist social system not as a single indivisible entity, we do not find capitalism's single two-class structure and only see multiple stratification instead. If we abandon it rather than just fail to adopt it—since the sociological dualism or multiplicity does, as argued in the introductory section of this essay, abandon an already existing noble and useful scientific tradition—if

we abandon the treatment of the capitalist system as a single indivisible entity we get a 'modification of the Marxian view'; and we
lose all sight of exploitation, of the consequent reciprocal and contradictory relation between development and underdevelopment,
and of the contradictory and antagonistic two-class structure. If this
were an essay in the sociology of knowledge, in the sociology of
modern sociology and ideology, we would at this point have to ask,
why Parsons and all those who share with him the *newly* conventional
wisdom so desire and insist on this abandonment of systemic theory,
this analytic breakdown of modern sociological analysis?

Stavenhagen's analysis does not suffer from Parsons' analytic
breakdown. He notes, that there is a capitalist unity, that it system-
atizes the relation to the means of production (which is often crudely
summarized as one of owners/non-owners), that this relation gives
rise to class, that consequently classes can only be said to exist with
respect to each other as part of the (capitalist) class system, that
because of its basis in the relation to the means of production the
class system necessarily involves class complementarity in the production process and class antagonism—which we have here termed
exploitation and that it is this class relation which is the mainspring
of social change.

Capitalism is then unitary but dialectic (dual but not in the sense
of the two separates of the dual society thesis but of a double sided
or sectored single system). Its structure and development is one of a
two-class antagonism, exploitation, and development-underdevelopment, overlaid by multiple social strata, diffusion, and degrees of
development. It is important indeed, to understand the connections
and relations between the single indivisible entity and its distinct
variables (to rely again on Parsons), between social class and social
stratification, between exploitation and diffusion, between underdevelopment and development, and between the relations among
class-exploitation-underdevelopment and those among stratification-
diffusion-development; but if it is important to understand these
relations, it is important not to confuse them as the conventional
wisdom systematically does.

Diffusion, stratification, and degrees of development (or underdevelopment) modify the visible aspects of exploitation, class conflict,
and the contradiction between development and underdevelopment;
but they do not alter, much less eliminate, the essential nature of

exploitation, class, and development/underdevelopment or of capitalism which is a collective name for them. It has been the intent of this essay to outline a perspective that may be of use in inquiring into the underlying structure of development and underdevelopment, of diffusion and exploitation, and to relate them with their varied and multiform manifestations as it is Stavenhagen's effort to inquire into the relation of the underlying class structure and the social stratification to which it gives rise.

Parsons notes, again correctly, that 'stratification is to an important degree an integrating structure in the social system' (Parsons 1954). That is, social stratification in a sense overlays the underlying class structure and, if it does not attenuate the exploitation and conflict between the two classes, it permits the system to persist despite that exploitation and conflict. Stavenhagen suggests that the stratification system is often in part a cultural lag still reflecting a class alignment which has shifted over time (without however losing its two-class antagonism). I would suggest, further, that the stratification system and the strata are in part the result and reflection of diffusion, especially from the upper to the lower class. That is, though the exploitative two-class structure persists, the upper class or 'bourgeoisie' diffuses to some members of the lower class or 'proletariat' some of the benefits of the former's exploitative position and gains. Without transforming these recipients into a part of the bourgeoisie itself, these economic, social, political, and cultural payoffs permit the bourgeoisie to obtain the co-operation of the recipients in the exploitative process and even to attenuate or eliminate their opposition to the exploitation or the underlying exploitative structure. These recipients are variously known as the petit bourgeoisie, middle class(es), aristocracy of the proletariat, etc. Far from eliminating it, the creation or existence of these strata, and the upper and lower ones with them, serves to perpetuate the exploitative class structure. They enlist more members of the system into the exploitative process, give these particular individuals an interest in maintaining it—though they themselves are exploited, and serve to substitute a stratification consciousness for class consciousness.

The consciousness of and fixation on stratification, of course, attenuates or even eliminates the perception of the essential contradictory structure of the capitalist system. Though conflict is not eliminated, it is dispersed, placing each person in actual or potential conflict with every other instead of concentrating conflict at the structural focus that gives rise to this conflict in the first place. Analogously and consequently as well, we may observe appearances of greater and lesser development, reflected in graded variations of income, occupational distribution, and other 'indexes of development' which far from eliminating the development-underdevelopment contradictions serve to maintain and even aggravate it—as do the tertiary sector middle classes.

The combination of the foregoing formulation of class and stratification, with the development-underdevelopment contradiction of capitalism as outlined below raises some further serious problems of analysis. It is one thing to say that capitalism has or is a two-class structure and another to say that there is only one single capitalist system in actual existence today, and it has two classes. Since throughout this essay I have been talking not only about capitalism as a form of social organization but about the particular capitalist system that began to form centuries ago and that today envelops the entire non-socialist world, I have to proceed to argue that there are only two classes in the capitalist world today, though there may be all kinds of strata.

Marxist analysis of the two-class structure of capitalism in no event is a matter of nose counting in order to pigeon-hole every observed person in his proper class such as that popularized by Lloyd Warner and others who seek to classify individuals or, to return to Parsons, identify distinct variables. Instead, Marxist analysis, and indeed any serious scientific analysis, devoted its primary theoretical attention to an anlysis of the structure of the system and not to a classification of its variables. In this sense, 'class' is primarily an analytic category which refers to the essential duality of capitalism, that of its contradictory, conflicting, exploiting class relation. The development-underdevelopment contradiction outlined in this essay has been intended in the same sense. Bourgeoisie/proletariat, development/underdevelopment are not primarily—in set theory language—sets or classes to which their members are to be assigned, but rather the dual conceptualization of the fundamental structure of capitalism.

Still, capitalism is not merely a conceptual category. There really is a capitalist system and there is, in fact, only one single capitalist system which embraces most of the world. Its essential structure, has given rise to real development and real underdevelopment. And the existence and development of this real capitalist system involves a real class antagonism throughout the capitalist world. How can we understand this contradictory and exploitative class relation and its manifestation through the stratification system(s) and through development and underdevelopment? I don't really know. But I shall try to make a few observations and suggestions related to this problem.

Are the peasants a class? Marx asked. His own answers, explicit and implicit in various parts of his written work, were not mutually consistent. Those of Marxists have been still less so. First of all, let me note that this question has Warnerian classificatory tones. The principal task is not perhaps to ask or to answer if all these particular people whom we define as peasants are a class by themselves or which class they are members of. Capitalism and *this* capitalist system has a two-class structure: not a three- or multi-class one. If this capitalist system involves the peasants, it does so in and through its two-class structure. There is no third class of peasants. There may be people in the world at one time or another who are not effective participants in and who are not incorporated in, the world capitalist system. Capitalism's class structure would, did, and does not affect these people. But there are no such people, to speak of, outside the socialist countries in the world today. There have not been many for a long time. (It will be important to analyse how and to what extent— if it is a matter of degree—the socialist countries have managed to get back out of the world capitalist system). Rejecting the 'dual society' thesis means denying that the peasants are outside of the capitalist system. They are, hence, part of this capitalist system's two class structure.

We may then ask: where are the peasants in the class structure? More specifically and more accurately, how do the peasants participate in this world capitalist system's two-class structure? They are exploited. They suffer from capitalist produced development. The peasants are not 'in a class by themselves'. The exploitative, development-underdevelopment, two-class structure of capitalism, of this capitalist system, affects, adversely we might say, all sorts of people in many parts of the stratification system(s). The occupational role, social status, political influence and cultural level of those who participate within the capitalist system as the exploited, display the widest variety from one person to the other. These differences among and within peasants, workers, students, clerks, loafers, buyers, sellers, do not eliminate the exploitative two-class, developed-under-developed structure of the capitalist system. They only perpetuate it and affect the course of the system's development.

How many class systems, how many two-class structures, are there? How many real capitalist systems are there on this globe to-day—or yesterday? There can be only one two-class structure, there is only one capitalist system. There may be Frenchmen, and Ceylo-nese, Tamils and Quetchuas, Argentinians and Yoruba. But there is no French proletariat, Tamil proletariat, Ceylonese bourgeoisie, Argentinian bourgeoisie in the sense of each having an existence independent of the other. What makes some Frenchmen 'members of' the bourgeoisie, or of the proletariat, or some Argentines or Ceylonese, is their relation to others as it is determined by the man-ner of their participation in the capitalist system, in the only one there is, the world-wide one. There is no doubt that in this world system, there are identifiable different industries, different enter-prises, each with an internal organization which determines directly for it as it does not for others some of the ways in which it participates in the system as a whole; and the same is the case also for states, nations, cultures, tribes, families, and other institutions; but that does not eliminate or even mitigate their participation in a single system which in one way or another relates them all. These organiza-tional factors only channel, concentrate, or disperse the diffusionary and exploitative relations to which the entire capitalist system and its participants are subject.

It may be asked whether all this is any more than playing with words. How does this formulation, as distinct from some other, affect the perception, understanding,—and transformation, of social rea-lity, especially of the underdeveloped countries? It does not provide any predetermined schematic or classificatory answers to such ques-tions as, 'is the American worker a member of the proletariat' (con-sidering that he may be exploited by the bourgeoisie but participates, may be, in the fruits of the exploitation of Brazilian peasants) or 'is the Brazilian industrialist a member of the bourgeoisie?' (given that he exploits Brazilian workers but is himself exploited by the metro-pole), or to the extensions of this question to practical politics, how do we treat the American worker and the Brazilian industrialist given that we want to transform or preserve (as the case may be) the system? This formulation in fact gives no answers at all to questions about specific aspects of reality at particular times and places, or to questions of what to do about them in specific situations. Nor does any worthwhile theory todate. It can only orient, adequately or not, our perception or inquiry into the structure or cause of social reality and to guide, thereby, our observation and action with respect to its particular manifestations. To note that peasants, industrialists, workers, the world over are all tied into a single system which makes all of them participate in one way or another in an exploitative process and relations, as exploiters or exploited or both and that this exploitation is at the heart of underdevelopment is likely to result in a different perception of and reaction to specific aspects of social reality than supposing that many peasants are systematically unrelated to other people.

There is no universally valid rule which permits us to detail the specific manifestations especially complicated by stratification and other social and cultural relations as they are, of the exploitative, two-class, development-underdevelopment producing structure of capitalism at all times and places. But we may—no, must—try to identify and understand the specific manifestations of the structure of the social system at some times and places.

I shall hazard some superficial generalizations about some class relations and their impact on development and underdevelopment based on observation of contemporary reality in Latin America. Really, a monograph or more is needed for each sentence and referring to each specific situation. Still, other—but different and I think mistaken—generalizations of a similar level abound already. That may justify the addition of still further ones if mine are more nearly true. Maybe the real justification lies only in the manner of constructing such generalization and in the adequacy of their application. Let us begin with a composite caricature of some conventional generalizations.

It is sometimes held that the peasants, or many of them, are here or there, out(side) of the class structure. Really that their masters, the feudal or pre-capitalist landlords, are also out of it. That both form their own class system, one for each country or even province on the map. There is a capitalist market-system rather confined to the political boundaries of this country; and another one confined to that country. There is a world market or an imperialism which affects these national capitalist systems in that it sort of reaches in with its long arm of trade investment, exploitation, etc. But the class system is rather confined to the country under discussion. It includes especially a working class, a bourgeois capitalist or business class (depending on terminology), and a growing middle class. Your development strategy depends on your political persuasion. Almost everybody from the reactionary right to the progressive left agrees that one of the best things to do is to have the middle classes grow as fast as possible. Gino Germani proposes, in an article in a scholarly journal, a 'Strategy for Stimulating Social Mobility' as in turn a development and stabilizing strategy (Germani 1972). Most people, from the moderate conservative right through the Communist Parties support a land reform which is supposed to eliminate feudalism, carry through or complete 'the bourgeois revolution', and 'incorporate the backward agriculture into the modern capitalist market/system.'

There is greater disagreement about the effects of 'foreign capital' or 'imperialism' and therefore what should be done about it, though there is really substantial agreement about its essential nature. The one argues that since capital is scarce in the underdeveloped country (by their definition), it should be attracted and welcomed. The other maintains that the foreigners take out more than they put in and that what they put in distorts the national development: accordingly foreign interests and influence should be eliminated. Both view the world market and 'foreign capital' or 'imperialism' as a sort of third sector, like a sort of second wing similar to that of agriculture attached to the national capitalist economic body. The one, all agree should be attached more firmly and the other, depending on persuasion, maintained or cut off.

The more conservative strategy is to perform the appropriate operation on the agricultural and foreign wings of the national economy and paying a minimum for the political support necessary. The Communist Party strategy is to ally themselves with that part of the bourgeoisie, the 'national' or 'industrial' or 'progressive' bourgeoisie, which wants to incorporate the peasants into and kick the foreigners out of the national capitalist economic body; and to reap the political rewards from this support, which in the short run are better wages, etc. for the C.P.-led political force, the workers, and in the long run are supposed to be the ability to take the leadership of the whole process away from the bourgeoisie and put it into the hands of the workers.

If the formulation of development-underdevelopment and class relations under contemporary capitalism advanced in this essay and this section are in the main correct, then the generalizations just summarized or caricatured are, despite their wide currency, in the main wrong for most countries of the underdeveloped world. Imperialism and agriculture are not wings or sectors of the national economy which can be more firmly attached or cut off at will without changing the fundamental capitalist structure of that national economy.

In fact, though there are state generated organizational discontinuities within the world capitalist system, there are in a very real and important sense no 'national' economies at all. There are only national sectors of a world capitalist economy. Moreover, agriculture and rural society in the various countries are not so many separate, and self-determining, sectors—neither are subsistence agriculture or feudal provincial society—but they are quite integral sectors of the economy and society as a whole. And their members participate as fully in the class structure as anybody else. A political or economic policy of 'penetrating' the 'feudal' or 'pre-capitalist' sector and 'incorporating' it into the 'national economy' is pure nonsense. That happened long ago. A policy of 'liberating' the national capitalist economy from imperialism is folly. That can't be done.

It may be possible to gain something analytically useful in describing the underdeveloped countries as the proletarian nations. Pierre Moussa (1959) calls them that in his book *Les Nations Proletaires*, but he does not treat them that way or, therefore, get any analytic mileage out of it. That would imply that the developed countries are the bourgeois ones, that they are indeed all part of the same capitalist system, and that this system involves them in an exploitative relation with each other. That need not imply that the bourgeoisie is not to be found in the underdeveloped countries or the proletariat in the developed ones. But it raises the question as to how the organization of the world capitalist system's productive process determined various groupings and their economic, social, political situations, and the manner of their participation in the continued transformation and/or elimination of the system. (Of course, it is not necessary to have recourse to the proletarian-bourgeois formulations to raise these questions).

Turning to the underdeveloped countries, specifically to those of Latin America, I may hazard the following general observations. The proletariat includes most of the participants in the economic system. It most certainly includes the peasants, 'subsistence' peasants included. Also the steadily employed workers, casually employed workers be they urban or rural (in case one doesn't want to call the latter 'peasants'), most of the members of the 'middle classes,', urban and rural. In today's underdeveloped countries, probably, ownership of the means of production is a better index of the bourgeoisie than it is in the metropolitan countries where corporate control has come to play a relatively greater role—except for instances of public ownership which far from indicating popular ownership, is a mechanism which permits the bourgeoisie to harvest the fruits of the public industry or sector while leaving the costs and risks of ownership to be borne by the people.

The examination of underdevelopment in various earlier sections of this essay suggests that the capitalist productive organization in the underdeveloped countries relegates owners of large scale land, domestic trade, international commerce, industry, finance, all together to the bourgeoisie. (Not that there are no conflicts of interest between these any more than one can deny that there are such conflicts between, say, capitalists in the United States and in Germany or anywhere else). The same foregoing examination suggests, therefore, that the participation of these groups in the capitalist economic system relegates them to the bourgeoisie in company with those of other countries, both under-developed and developed. In other words, *by virtue of their relation in the productive process to the proletariat, these capitalists in one underdeveloped country are allied to analogous ones elsewhere and to the bourgeoisie in the remainder of the periphery and in the metropole.*

It is not their economic relation with each other which allies and unites these diverse capitalist groups and sub-groups, for that of course tends to divide them into conflicting interests groups; it is their exploitative relation to others which allies and unites them in spite of their conflicting interests. The less the current economic or political activity of the proletariat threatens them, the more will their mutually conflicting interests determine the form of the economic and political process. On the other hand, the more the activity of the proletariat—and of the socialist system which has escaped from the bourgeoisie's exploitation—threatens the exploitative basis of their participation in the productive process, the more does their common exploitative interest determine their policy.

This double tendency may be observed among bourgeois interest groups within the metropole, and within the periphery and its various parts, and among all of them put together. It is not any innate co-operativeness or love for each other that makes the metropolitan bourgeoisie and the peripheral comprador bourgeoisie, national industrial bourgeoisie—(if it exists) and the feudal landowners combine forces, especially when the chips are down; it is the common threat to them all which arises out of their common participation in the productive process as exploiters of the proletariat. Collectively they cannot help it, however much they might like to—or however much certain members or representatives of the proletariat might like them to.

Capitalism and Development/Underdevelopment

Only the briefest summary statement of the analysis and thesis of this essay should now be necessary. Underdevelopment, no less than development itself, is the product but also part of the motive power of capitalism. Capitalist development everywhere has been a fundamentally contradictory development based on exploitation and resulting simultaneously in development and underdevelopment. Additionally, the growth and expansion of European mercantilism of the 16th century led to the development of a single, integrated, capitalist system of world-wide scope. Associated ever since the very beginning with the growth of powerful states, the expansion of mercantilism-capitalism led to the development of a metropole and, related to it through ties of commerce and force, of a periphery. Variously related to each other through colonialism, free-trade, imperialism, and 'neo-colonialism' the metropole exploited the periphery in such a way and extent that the metropole became what we today call developed while the periphery became what we now call underdeveloped.

At the same time, the same fundamental contradiction of capitalism led to a development/underdevelopment structure within the metropole and its regional and sectoral parts and within the various national and regional parts of the periphery. These national development/underdevelopment contradictions differ from the global one primarily in that, in addition to reflecting the inevitable exploitative structure of capitalism anywhere, they are additionally subordinate to, and in large part a consequence of, the contradictory exploitative-development/underdevelopment structure of the single world-wide capitalist-colonialist-imperialist system which came to dominate most of the globe. Capitalism, and more particulary the single world capitalist system and its various national sectors, has not changed, as it cannot change, its fundamental contradictory, exploitative structure and character. Accordingly, we may note, the development of development and the development of underdevelopment continues apace both on the global or international level and on the various national levels on which the capitalist system continues to operate. The only peoples who have been capable of escaping from underdevelopment are those who have substituted socialism for capitalism. Only the development of socialism has permitted any people already suffering from metropolitan produced peripheral underdevelopment to escape from the structure of the world capitalist system and from its consequent underdevelopment.

All serious study of the problems of development of underdeveloped areas and all serious intent to formulate policy for the elimination of underdevelopment and for the promotion of development must take into account, nay must begin with, this fundamental historical and structural cause of underdevelopment in capitalism. Indeed, all serious study of development must take into account the fundamental relation the development of development has had, and continues to have, with the development of underdevelopment. All serious study of capitalism, of its manifestation in the development of the metropole and of that in the underdevelopment of the periphery, and especially the study of the contemporary single world capitalist system and its development in the past and future, must begin with capitalism's unity and its fundamental internal contradiction, which has always and everywhere expressed itself in diffusion and exploitation, development and underdevelopment.

The conventional wisdom about underdevelopment, its causes, and its elimination are entirely inadequate. The reasons have been

detailed above. Each of several central tenets of the conventional
wisdom are quite out of keeping with past and contemporary reality.
Thus, the conventional notion that underdevelopment is 'initial'
and 'traditional' is evidently challenged by all historical fact and
observation. Yet, whatever the differences among various branches
or modes of conventional analysis, the notion of underdevelopment
as an initial state is explicitly or implicitly common to it all.

Inadequate also is the idea that development is a process while
underdevelopment is a state of being. And erroneous is the associated
supposition that development occurred essentially independently
in that the now developed areas took off and left the now underdeveloped ones behind where they were. The evidence is that the
development of the former occurred in conjunction with underdevelopment and at the cost of the latter; both development and
underdevelopment were and are processes; more accurately, they
were and are both part of the same process. Similarly unsupported
by the examination of the historical evidence is the popular and
in the conventional wisdom well nigh universal notion that having
taken off independently, the metropole now does or will diffuse out
or trickle down to the periphery the wherewithal necessary for the
underdeveloped countries to develop as well. The evidence of the
past and present is that far from diffusing down development, the
relation between the metropole and periphery widens the gap
between the two and generates ever deeper structural underdevelopment in the periphery.

All of these tenets of the conventional wisdom neglect or deny
that there exists a single social and economic system which
embraces everybody in the non-socialist world, including the most
'isolated' 'subsistence' farmer, and that it is in the structure and
operation of this system that we must seek all the essentials of development and underdevelopment. The conventional wisdom, and
many would–be Marxists as well, instead have adopted a dualist or
multiple sociology which claims to identify, especially in the underdeveloped periphery, dual societies whose two or more supposed
parts are essentially independent of each other. One or more of
these, then, are termed as exhibiting the social, economic, political,
cultural, etc. 'structure' of underdevelopment *within* it, while another
one is termed 'developed' in that it exhibits some of the features of
the metropolitan economy and society. Development is then quite

erroneously and inadequately viewed as the diffusion of development from this national metropolitan centre out to the underdeveloped provincial periphery—or rather the re-diffusion of what has already been diffused down or out from the global metropole. Sometimes, this process is regarded less in terms of diffusion than in terms of the penetration of the capitalist metropole into the 'pre-capitalist' or 'feudal' periphery, or again, the incorporation of the pre-capitalist sector into the more developed capitalist one.

The evidence belies the existence of such a process. Far from being due to the existence and operation in the underdeveloped peripheral provinces of a feudal or pre-capitalist system, a careful reading of the historical and contemporary evidence demonstrates that what goes on there today is the result of these people's incorporation in the capitalist system long ago, albeit admittedly not into its developing but rather into its underdeveloping sector. Any 'development' policy will therefore surely and necessarily be inadequate if it rests on the supposition that underdevelopment can be eliminated in the peripheral area in question by eliminating 'pre-capitalism' or 'feudalism' and substituting capitalism instead—that is, more of the same capitalism which caused the underdevelopment and now maintains it. Serious study of the problems of development and underdevelopment will have to go well beyond the conventional wisdom.

This essay has been an attempt to re-examine in brief some of the evidence relating to underdevelopment and to suggest in only the most preliminary outline form some of the essentials of an alternative but more adequate approach to the examination, analysis, understanding, and conscious transformation or elimination of development, underdevelopment, and capitalism. This alternative approach rests on two fundamental pillars, historicity and structural unity. Though the development of my own thinking has so far been based almost entirely on (re) examination of the evidence, the conceptual framework I have distilled out of this study is really quite classical. Though widely employed in part by the classical economists (structural unity of a single system) and the German (historical) school and still honoured in principle if less so in practice by many social scientists today, the most intensive and fruitful reliance on this approach to date has been that of Marx and some of his followers.

In contrast to others, excepting some though by no means

all of his followers, Marx added, or rather noted, a further matter however: he noted the dialectical nature of the historical process and its structural unity, and he incorporated them into his analysis. In the foregoing examination and analysis of social reality, we have repeatedly seen that the unity of the single capitalist system and the history of its development are fraught with fundamental, seemingly inescapable, contradictions which account for the very development/underdevelopment problem that has been the subject of our study itself. And we have found the problems of development and underdevelopment to be inseparable from the development of capitalism to which no one before or since Marx has devoted the intensive study that he did. In seeking to develop an approach or method of study and analysis of the contemporary problems of development and underdevelopment in the capitalist world it is therefore well to return to, the method of Marx.

In relying on Marx as well as on contemporary observation and analysis, it is above all his method, more so than his particular studies of the past or predictions about the future, that will serve us. In that, of course, the most important contribution of Marx is like that of any other scientist: it is his method, not his particular study, related though they may be, that can help other scientists the most. Writing where and when he did, Marx's reliance on historical development, on materialist determination (though not of course as many of his defamers claim on a materialist ethic), on dialectical contradiction, on a single integrated—though contradiction ridden—system and its development emphasized the development of capitalism and focused on the metropole and especially England. And he emphasized, of course, the development of an exploiting bourgeoisie and an exploited proletariat as integral and necessary parts of the development of capitalism.

Our emphasis and focus, writing after a further 100 years of capitalist development and expressing a concern especially with the underdeveloped periphery of the world which shapes the lives of most of its people, will not be the same as that of Marx, or even that of Lenin who wrote before some of the 19th century tendencies had borne all the fruits they have today—including the creation of a socialist world. When we think in terms of 'system' and of its integration and unity, we may look at the globe as a whole and note that it has been embraced by a single integrated capitalist system. When we look at past events, and more important at their historical inter-relation and the development to which that gave rise (which is not the same), we may look at the development of capitalism on a world scale; and we may note that in important respects this began in mercantilist days long before Britain's industrialization. In looking at the historical development of a single capitalist system we shall not see only the industrialization of Britain or the development of the metropole, but we shall find the expansion and development of a world-scale capitalist system. The exploitation of the proletariat by the bourgeoisie that Marx analysed so well for Britain may appear in the form of the exploitation of the periphery by the metropole as well.

The dialectic contradictory development of capitalism discussed by Marx, may also reappear in the contradiction between the developed metropole and the underdeveloped periphery, no less than it does in the class conflict between the bourgeoisie and the proletariat in the metropole itself. And the chain of exploitative and diffusionist class relations within the metropole and between the metropole and the farthest reaches of the periphery may be con-gruent with the chain of development/underdevelopment contradic-tions that reach from the metropole of the metropole to the peri-phery of the periphery via the various peripheries of the metropole and metropoles of the periphery. Similarly, the motive force that Marx understood to be in the diffusionist-exploitative contradictions of capitalism and which he identified in the class struggle within the metropole may now be increasingly identified in the contradiction between the developed metropole and the underdeveloped peri-phery, plus the socialist sector which has escaped from the exploita-tion and underdevelopment of the capitalist-imperialist system. Indeed socialism may appear less as the dynamic response of the metropolitan proletariat to its exploitation than as that of the peri-pheral part of the system in the underdeveloped countries. As in 1914 the problem of co-operation and unity among sectors of the metropolitan proletariat arose and was resolved in well known ways, now the problem may arise of the relation among the prole-tariat in the developed metropole and in the underdeveloped peri-phery and with the forces of the socialist world.

Capitalism and Socialism

Socialism may be regarded as the historical response to the development of development and underdevelopment resulting from
capitalist exploitation. Marx predicted that the increasing tension
that capitalism produced between the exploited and their exploiters
will result in the destruction, by the exploited, of the system that
generates this exploitation and in its replacement by socialism.
Looking at particular capitalist countries, the internal capitalist
contradiction might appear to become most acute in the most industrialized one. We have noted before that, simultaneously, Marx
thought that industrialization would on the other hand 'trickle down'
from England to India. Blessed by hindsight as we are, we might
now say that history has unfolded in more Marxian terms than
Marx himself foresaw. Development has not trickled down from the
developed to the underdeveloped countries, nor could it have if
previous historical experience and/or the fundamentals of Marxist
theory (rather than particular predictions of Marxists—including
Marx) are any indication. The contradiction between the exploited
and their exploiters, between underdevelopment and development,
has instead become greater and deeper.

Looking at the capitalist system on a world scale the conflict between the bourgeoisie and the proletariat in the metropole appears
as only one aspect of capitalist exploitation, which now takes the
relation between the metropole and the periphery, between development and underdevelopment, as its principal and most acute
form. It is in the periphery, then, that the principal struggle for
emancipation from this exploitation, from dependent underdevelopment takes place. (We may note that, if the entire argument of this
essay is well taken, it is not the case, as is often said, that this struggle
is not taking place in that part of the capitalist system that is most
developed. On the contrary, if we remember that the fullest development of capitalism results in the greatest contradiction between
development and underdevelopment, we may note that the contemporary struggle by the exploited in the periphery takes place precisely where—structurally—capitalist 'development,' has had its most
oppressive effects).

Marx argued that the emancipation from capitalist exploitation
would involve the destruction and abandonment of the system of

capitalist relations to the means of production. Capitalism would be followed by socialism. History has so far proved him right; and the present analysis, like his, suggests that it could not be otherwise. The review of the evidence in the pages above showed that, so far, no national, or other sector of the world capitalist system, once underdeveloped, has been able to escape from underdevelopment and still preserve capitalist productive relations. No such country has so far been able to liberate itself from imperialism, or from underdevelopment, through reliance on a 'national capitalism,' led by a 'national bourgeoisie.' Many have tried. All have failed. We have reviewed the several attempts of Chile in the 19th century. Argentina tried. So did Paraguay. (For reviews of these latter cases of 'frustrated development' see for instance, Jorge Abelardo Ramos, *América Latina: Un Pais* 1949). So did Brazil. And so may be interpreted — or reinterpreted if necessary — the history of several other countries.

It would be interesting to argue whether, in principle, it would have been possible at that time to escape national underdevelopment through independent capitalism, even though it would have involved the recreation of the exploitative development/underdevelopment structure of the metropolitan countries in an experipheral one, and even though it would have transformed such a country into another metropolitan — that is imperialist — one. We shall never know since 19th century imperialism quite efficiently frustrated all these attempts, sometimes already quite well advanced, at independent capitalist development. (I remind the reader that Japan, which may seem to be a counter example only further proves the rule since it had not been colonialized or underdeveloped — prior to its independent development. Moreover, as the post World War II period shows, Japan was eventually also unable to escape the capitalist — imperialist fate).

We have also noted that there have been several attempts during contemporary times to escape from imperialism and underdevelopment through independent national capitalism. All have failed. There will be renewed attempts. They will fail as well. It has not been possible to disentangle a national economy from the world capitalist one as long as the national one remained capitalist as well. I have tried to suggest in the preceding pages why this appears to have been necessary on theoretical grounds. No 'national bourgeoisie' has been able, in the long run, to liberate itself — to say nothing of its nations's people — from the world capitalist-imperialist bourgeoisie.

Only the elimination of the capitalist structure, within a certain territory and among a certain people, and its substitution by socialist ones has so far offered any escape either from imperialism or from underdevelopment. The destruction of capitalism and the introduction of socialism may then, from the point of view of the problem examined in this essay, be regarded so far as the only. possible escape from imperialism and from underdevelopment. Socialism may be regarded, then, as the continuance of the historical process which through capitalist expansion and development has produced development and underdevelopment and which requires the development of mankind into socialism in order to avoid still further underdevelopment. Notable, in this connection is the fact that all the countries which have turned to socialism indeed were part of the capitalist exploited underdeveloped periphery before doing so. It is equally notable that in the one country, the Soviet Union, in which socialism has so far had a, still short, but not very brief existence, imperialism-colonialism and underdevelopment, both of the U.S.S.R. itself and of its regions and peoples, has by general agreement been eliminated.

Certainly the impact of socialist development in the U.S.S.R. on Central Asia, which were underdeveloping capitalist internal colonies during Czarist times, has been quantitatively and qualitatively altogether different from the experience of any external or internal peripheral underdeveloped colony which has remained in the capitalist system. So far, both the Eastern European and the Asian post World War II newcomers to socialism hold out adequate promise of achieving the same liberation and development or more. The possible exception is Yugoslavia, which the Chinese are now (1963) terming non-socialist. Notably, Yugoslavia has become reinvolved to a quite substantial degree in the world imperialist system. (It is to be understood that throughout this discussion I do not use the term 'socialist' for practitioners of 'Indian-,' 'Arab-,' or 'African' socialism who have never escaped from the imperialist — or capitalist — system to begin with).

The foregoing formulation has serious political implications. It implies, in Marxist terms, that the fundamental contradiction today is the capitalist one between development and underdevelopment, including that between the bourgeoisie and the proletariat and that the contradiction between capitalism and socialism is a derived and secondary one. Contemporary official Soviet interpretation accuses the Chinese of officially taking the position that the under-development-development contradiction predominates over the capitalist-socialist one (see, for instance the famous 'Open Letter' in *Pravda* in answer to the Chinese '25 Points'). The Chinese, in their important document 'More on the Differences between Comrade Togliatti and Us' do appear to take the former position on one page and to affirm that... (manuscript illegible).... (The study of) underdevelopment leads, to the position that capitalist development-underdevelopment is the primary contradiction, though it leads also, of course, to the conclusion that combating imperialism and turning to socialism are its only possible resolution.

Capitalism and Liberation

The foregoing review and analysis of the development of under-development as the necessary consequences of the development of capitalism lead inevitably to the conclusion that the abandonment of capitalism and the substitution of socialism must constitute the most important essential of any real development policy for under-developed countries today. Without attempting to set out a development policy for all times and places in detail, the outlines of the essentials of such policy, as they are derived from the foregoing analysis, may be set out in brief.

We have seen that underdevelopment is the apparently inevitable result of the historical development of capitalism over the past few centuries. Not only did underdevelopment develop as a consequence of the development of capitalism in the past, but the process continues and repeats itself today. It continues in the sense that the development of the world capitalist system continues to produce metropolitan development and peripheral underdevelopment today as it has in the past, continues to deepen the contradiction between the two and to deepen and strengthen the structure of underdevelopment itself. It repeats past experience in the sense that renewed attempts in the periphery to liberate one country or another from th-

underdevelopment consequent upon the operation of the imperia-
list-capitalist system are repeatedly frustrated by that very same
imperialist system today as they were in the past; and each such
frustrated attempt at development leaves a new residue of structural
underdevelopment that will be much more costly to overcome
in the future. The only way out of underdevelopment is the way out
of the system that produces, maintains, and aggravates it; it is the
way out of the world capitalist system.

The evidence and any adequate theoretical analysis of the operation of the contemporary world capitalist system demonstrate that
even the independence of a national capitalist system is prohibited
by the structure and operation of the world capitalist-imperialist
system. A particularly important consequence of this dependence of
national capitalism on imperialism is the essential dependence of the
'national bourgeoisie' in this or that underdeveloped country on
imperialism. Notwithstanding all the conflicts of interest that undoubtedly do exist between a Brazilian or an Indian national industrial bourgeoisie and imperialism and its direct domestic clients and
agents, the structure of international capitalism—of imperialism—
and of national capitalism do not permit such a bourgeoisie to lead
an independent national development. Insofar as that bourgeoisie's
essential exploitative position is directly or indirectly threatened by
the action of the proletariat in its country and/or of socialism elsewhere, that bourgeoisie is necessarily all the more allied to imperialism's foreign and domestic agents. If this lack of national independence exists in countries and for bourgeoisies with as strong a
'developed' industrial sector as India and Brazil and as great a
resource potential, then it is all the more so the case in countries
elsewhere in Asia, Latin America, and most especially in the 'new'
nations of Africa, which cannot boast a 'national' bourgeoisie, other
than in the sense that the would be commercial interests of some
peripheral country would like to replace some of their foreign
competitors in the ' enefits of the very same exploitative commercial
sector. But if the bourgeoisie, national or otherwise—not to speak of
imperialism itself as the conventional 'trickle down,' diffusionist
wisdom does—cannot liberate underdeveloped countries today from
underdevelopment, then only the proletariat—and those already
liberated by socialism—can do it.

The development strategy of the proletariat must be to destroy capitalism and unseat the bourgeoisie in its country and to substitute and develop a socialist structure instead. To take its country out of the underdevelopment producing imperialist system, it must eliminate capitalism in the country. In previous phases of historical development it has sometimes been possible for gradual economic changes to precede political ones which only, so to say, then ratify and consolidate the economic transformation. This was the case because a second exploitative minority grew up alongside an existing one and then replaced the first one, though not exploitation itself. I say 'sometimes' because, though this is the classical model of the French revolution in particular and capitalist development in the metropole in general, it is not what occurred, in general, in the substitution of capitalism for pre-existing forms in the periphery. That was a political act, though based on economic changes in the metropole, from the very beginning. And it, as well a. 'he maintenance of the 'liberal' economic, political, social, and cultural relations which it introduced in the periphery, was, as Frantz Fanon so poignantly points out in *The Wretched of the Earth*, an act of force and violence. Be that as it may, this pattern of development was altered with the Soviet October Revolution which, though of course also based on pre-existing transformations in the economic structure, confirmed the primacy of political transformation. That is, its political action in the Soviet Union did not confirm a new exploitative economic structure at the expense of an old one but it laid the basis, rather, for the development of an economic structure which no longer permitted or necessitated the unrequited exploitation of the majority by a minority. At the same time, as we observed above, the Soviet Revolution was also the first emancipation of an underdeveloped peripheral country from capitalist-imperialist produced underdevelopment. All liberation movements which have since then successfully emancipated their people from imperialism-capitalism and from the structure of underdevelopment have similarly been political movements which have encountered but overcome the force and violence of the defenders of capitalism which has characterized capitalism's implantation and maintenance in the periphery from the beginning.

A member of the Indian Planning Commission notes that history provides not one single example in which liberation from the structure of underdevelopment has been achieved without violence. But, he says, he and other Indians have 'faith' that in India it can and will be achieved. Faith it is, for neither evidence nor theory provide any other basis for thinking—or even hoping—so. Thus any development strategy which is not based solely on blind faith must rest in the first instance on political means and those who would really achieve the liberation of their people from underdevelopment must be prepared to meet violent resistance to their political policy. Indeed, as Frantz Fanon observes, they have been meeting it all along, since the entire colonial status quo rests on the violence of the metropole and its domestic agents. The necessary political strategy for development is, of course, the destruction of capitalism or the elimination of that country from the world capitalist system.

Since the development strategy of the proletariat—including especially the peasants—must be to eliminate capitalism and the bourgeoisie to which it gives rise, any alliance with the bourgeoisie or its parts, is very dangerous. This includes not only, of course, the metropolitan bourgeoisie—that is 'imperialism'—or its domestic 'comprador' client-agent but the so called 'national' bourgeoisie as well. Not that the proletariat should not seek to take advantage of intra-bourgeois conflicts and through temporary alliance with one or another of its sectors try to contribute to the weakening of the bourgeoisie at home or abroad as a whole. It should if it can. But such alliances cannot but serve to retard the possibilities of escaping from underdevelopment, and worse to undermine them, if instead of weakening the bourgeoisie it strengthens it or strengthens it more than it strengthens the power of the proletariat to finally destroy it.

But that has been the result of innumerable well meant proletarian alliances with the national bourgeoisie, as the Chinese experience with the Kuomintang in Shanghai in 1927 and dozens of cases of Communist Party—bourgeoisie alliances in Latin America have demonstrated. These left the bourgeoisie stronger than before, strong enough immediately to renounce its alliance with the Communist Party, and more entrenched so as better to resist all future popular attempts at liberating the country from underdevelopment—though not strong enough to resist its renewed or increased submission by the imperialist system. Many of these popular alliances were of course based on the erroneous notion that the 'national' bourgeoisie really has possibilities of independent action in the long run. Abandonment of this notion and improved comprehension of how the capitalist system actually works would undoubtedly shift many potential future

108   on capitalist underdevelopment

such alliances from the 'probably advantageous' to the probably or certainly disadvantageous—even disastrous, category.

This last consideration, popular action or inaction which contributes the strengthening of the bourgeoisie and to further consolidation of capitalist development in the periphery, is of special importance today in the parts of the already underdeveloped periphery, especially of Africa but of Latin America and Asia as well, in which industry, and therefore a relatively strong 'national' bourgeoisie, does not yet, or no longer, exist. The 'progressive' branch of the conventional wisdom in the West, but much of Marxist thinking as expressed especially through the Communist Parties associated with the Moscow strategy of national liberation, is to encourage the growth and fortification of these national bourgeoisies. More often than not the bourgeoisies are not national in the classical Communist Party sense of being industrially based instead of 'comprador', but are so only in the sense of being the less reactionary wing of a group of nationals who rise to challenge or replace foreigners in some commercial and political positions associated with the country's peripheral colonialized/imperialized relationship to the metropole.

Possibly no stronger argument against confiding the leadership of the periphery's people to, or confiding in, *these* bourgeoisies (or in the terms of this essay, members of the bourgeoisie) exists than that of Frantz Fanon to whose *The Wretched of the Earth* anyone seriously concerned with the development of the colonialized underdeveloped countries must return again and again. Quite consistently with the analysis outlined in this essay, Fanon argues that these bourgeoisies must necessarily divert the process of national liberation from the system which produces underdevelopment into a prolongation of colonialism through other forms. He notes also, as I have above, that the introduction of the liberal party and electoral system— even in its increasingly popular one-party form—can only serve as an instrument of this continued exploitative and underdevelopment maintaining relation. Worse, their participation in the commercial and political institutional apparatus of capitalism and neocolonialism only corrupts the new members of the bourgeoisie and, through the bureaucratic and electoral apparatus especially, the urban petit bourgeoisie or middle classes insofar as they are not already corrupted by capitalism and colonialism/imperialism to begin with.

But the analysis outlined above leads to a further important observation which seems to have escaped Fanon at least in part. He says at one point that once this bourgeoisie has been eaten up by its own internal contradictions (or I might add those it develops with the metropole) and has shown itself incapable of really emancipating its people, it will be evident that 'nothing has happened since independence, that it is necessary to redo everything, that it is necessary to start again at zero.' But the fundamentals of Fanon's own analysis, like the one outlined here, suggest that it will certainly not be possible to begin again at zero as though nothing had transpired, and that most probably it will be necessary to begin again at a point more underdeveloped than zero. Fanon himself alludes several times to the good lesson but horrible example that the sad experience of 150 years of Latin American liberty under 'liberalism' portend for Africa. But Latin America and all the rest of the periphery including Africa demonstrate that history, and especially the development of underdevelopment, do not permit us to start again at zero. We can only 'start again' where history has left us off.

The question arises, where and how would or will another period of capitalist development and underdevelopment leave these underdeveloped countries. The argument of the trickling down diffusionists of course is that it will leave them more developed. Even Marx argued that Bismarck—in a different but analogous situation—was 'doing some of our work for us' in unifying Germany and consolidating its bourgeoisie. Maybe, but Marx's harvest time of these fruits has not yet come in West Germany 100 years later. Be that as it may, it is important to understand, as the entire review and analysis of this essay suggests, that in the periphery especially another period of bourgeois-led capitalist development also deepens underdevelopment. That seems to be a consideration which is left out of account by those who argue that 'give the Soviet Union 20 more years of industrial development and it (we) will be strong enough to help everybody liberate himself from imperialism and develop.' The question is, of course, whether this further period of capitalism in the periphery will increase its development possibilities more than it increases its structural underdevelopment. All technological progress, diffusion, internal transformation in the metropole—and if recent events are any guide even in parts of the socialist world—notwithstanding, the historical evidence evidently does not serve as the basis for any hope that another period of capitalism will improve the possibilities of development in the underdeveloped countries more than it will condemn them to still further underdevelopment. Both the evidence and our analysis point rather to the opposite—that is to further structural underdevelopment under capitalism produced through the economic, political, social, cultural, and maybe technological, process in the future as it has in the past.

There is of course one exception to this tendency, and it is an important one. Continued capitalist produced development and underdevelopment, as well as continued socialist development, will so deepen the contradiction that it will augment the pressure for its resolution. But at a cost very much higher than would be necessary for its resolution now. Inevitably, if the pressure and force of the liberation movement will increase, so will that of the capitalist status quo and its institutions. If rivers of blood are necessary for liberation from capitalism and underdevelopment now, oceans of blood may be necessary then. All the evidence, including nuclear development, suggests that with each year, on the national level and or the global one, the cost of liberation from underdevelopment rises. The strategy of liberation and development and the strategy for peace must indeed be, as some argue and the above analysis suggests, one of unity for liberation now, for the contrary strategy of liberation later very much increases the probability of veritable bloodbaths on the national level and/or a holocaust on the global one.

The argument of this essay is, thus, not an idle one. Arguing from the past, it goes to the heart of the future.

Bibliography[*]

Abelardo Ramos, Jorge 1949, *América Latina: Un País*, Buenos Aires, Editorial Octubre

Alavi, Hamza 1963, U.S. Aid to Pakistan, An Evaluation, *Economic Weekly* (Bombay) XV, July

Amin, Samir, 1974, *Accumulation on a World Scale*, New York and London, Monthly Review Press

—— 1973 *Le Développement Inégal*, Paris, Minuit

Arrighi, Giovanni and John S. Saul, 1972, *Essays on the Political Economy of Africa*, New York and London, Monthly Review Press

Bagú, Sergio 1949, *Economía de la sociedad colonial: Ensayo de la historia comparada de América Latina*, Buenos Aires, El Ateneo

Balandier, Georges 1956, *Le Tiers Monde Sous-développement et développement*, Paris, INED

Baran, Paul A. 1957, *The Political Economy of Growth*, New York, Monthly Review Press

Boeke, J. H. 1942, *The Structure of the Netherlands Indian Economy*, New York, Institute of Pacific Relations

—— 1953, *Economics and Economic Policy of Dual Societies*, New York, Institute of Pacific Relations

Cardoso, Fernando Henrique Y Enzo Faletto, 1970, *Dependencia y Desarrollo en América Latina*, Mexico Siglo XXI Editore

Coulborne, Rushton (ed.) 1956, *Feudalism in History*, Princeton, Princeton University Press

des Santos, Theotonio 1970, *Dependencia y Cambio Social*, Santiago CESO

Downs, Anthony 1957, *An Economic Theory of Democracy*, New York, Harper & Row

Dutt, R. Palme 1949, *India Today*, Bombay, People's Publishing House

Fanon, Frantz 1962, *Les Damnés de la Terre*, Paris, François Maspero *The Wretched of the Earth*, London, Penguin Books

Frank, André Gunder 1960 'The Michigan Economy—More Eggs in our Manufacturing Basket?' *Michigan Economic Record*, Vol. II, No. 4, July

—— in 1963, 'Brazil: Exploitation or Aid?' *The Nation* (New York), Nov. 16

—— in *Latin America: Underdevelopment or Revolution*, New York, Monthly Review Press 1970, Chapter 8

—— 1963 (now 1967, 1969), 'A agricultura brasileira: Capitalismo e o mito do feudalismo' *Revista Brasiliense* (Sao Paulo), No. 51, Jan.–Feb. 1964

—— 1967 *Capitalism and Underdevelopment in Latin America*, New York, Monthly

---

[*] The time that has elapsed since the writing of this essay and the geographical displacement of the author now make it impossible in some cases to give complete references to the works cited in the text.

Review Press, (revised and enlarged edition, 1969) London, Penguin Books 1971
——— 1970, *Latin America: Underdevelopment or Revolution*. New York, Monthly Review Press
Translation of Frondizi, Arturo 1958 *Política y Petróleo*, Buenos Aires
Furtado, Celso 1959 *A formacao económica do Brasil*, Rio de Janeiro, Fundo de Cultura
——— *The Economic Growth of Brazil*, Berkeley, University of California Press
— 1961 *Desenvolvimento y Subdesenvolvimento*, Rio de Janeiro, Fundo de Cultura
Germani, Gino 1962 *Política y Sociedad en una Epoca de transición*, Buenos Aires
1962 'Estrategia para estimular la movilidad social' *Desarrollo Económico* (Buenos Aires), Vol. I, No. 3
Goldschmidt, Arthur 1963 "Economic Development of the South," *Scientific American* (New York) September
Gonzáles Casanova, Pablo 1963 'Sociedad plural, colonialismo interno y desarrollo' *America Latina* (Rio de Janeiro) Año 6. No. 3
    Sociología de la explotación, México, Siglo XXI, 1969
Guyer, Robert E. 1952, *Imperialismo, Introduccion a su Problemática* Buenos Aires
Harris, Marvin 1959, 'The Economy has no Surplus?' *American Anthropologist* (Mennesha, Wisc.) No. 61
Hinkelammert, Franz, 1970 *Dialécrica del Desarrollo Desiqual*, Santiago, CEREN Universidad Catholica
Hirschmann, Albert 1958, *The Strategy of Economic Development*, New Haven, Yale University Press
Lacoste, Yves 1961, *Os Países Subdesenvolvidos*, Sao Paulo, Difusao Europea do Livro
——— *Les Pays Sous-Developpés*, Paris, P.U.F., Collection 'Que sais je?'
Lattimore, Owen 1960, 'The Industrial Impact on China, 1800-1950' *First International Conference of Economic History*, Stockholm 1960, The Hague, Mouton & Co.
Leibenstein, Harvey 1957, *Economic Backwardness and Economic Growth*, New York, John Wiley & Sons
Magdoff, Harry 1969, *The Age of Imperialism*, New York, Monthly Review Press
Manchester, Allan K. 1933 *British Pre-eminence in Brazil: Its Rise and Fall*, Chapel Hill, University of North Carolina Press
Marini, Rui Mauro, 1969 *Subdesarrollo v Revolución*, Mexico, Siglo XXI Editores, 5th revised ed, 1974
——— 1973, *La Dialéctica de la Dependencia*, Mexico, Ediciones Era
Marriott, McKim 1952, 'Technological Change in Overdeveloped Rural Areas,' *Economic Development and Cultural Change* (Chicago), Vol. 1, Dec.
Marx, Karl n.d. *On Colonialism*, Moscow, Foreign Languages Publishing House
Moussa, Pierre 1959, *Les Nations Proletaires*, Paris, Presses Universitaires de France
Myrdal, Gunnar 1944, *An American Dilemma*, New York, Harper & Brothers
——— 1957, *Economic Theory and Underdeveloped Regions*, London, Gerald Duckworth
Nabuco, Joaquim 1892, *Balmaceda*, Rio de Janeiro
Norman, E. Herbert 1940 *Japan's Emergence as a Modern State*, New York, Institute of Pacific Relations
Normano, J.F. 1931 *The Struggle for South America*, Boston, Houghton Mifflin
Palloix, Cristian 1974, *L'Economie Capitaliste Mondiale*, Paris, François Maspero Editeur, (2 vols.) 2nd ed.

Parsons, Talcott 1954 *Essays in Sociological Theory*, Glencoe, The Free Press, Revised Edition

Peking Review 1963, 'Is Yugoslavia a Socialist Country?'

Pinto, Aníbal 1958, *Chile: Un Caso de Desarrollo Frustrado*, Santiago, Ed. Universitaria

Polanyi, Karl 1944, *The Great Transformation*, New York, Reinhardt Holt

—— et al., 1957, *Trade and Markets in the Early Empires*, Glencoe, The Free Press

Prado Junior, Caio 1960, "Contribucao para a análise da questio agrária no Brasil" *Revista Brasiliense* (Sao Paulo) No. 28, Marzo-Abril

Prado Junior, Caio 1963, *Historia Económica de Brasil*, Sao Paulo, Editora Brasiliense, 7a. ed. Historia Económica del Brasil, Buenos Aires, Editora Futuro 1960

Prebisch, Raúl 1963, *Hacia una didamica del desarrollo Latinoamericano*, Naciones Unidas 680/Rev. 1 *Towards a Dynamic Development Policy for Latin America*, United Nations 680/Rev. 1

Prescott, Walter 1937, *Divided we Stand*

Ramirez Necochea, Hernán 1958, *Balmaceda y la contrarevolución de 1891*, Santiago, Ed. Universitaria

Rostow, Walt Whitman 1960, *The Stages of Economic Growth*, Cambridge, Cambridge University Press

Sahlins, Marshall D. 1958, *Social Stratification in Polynesia* Seattle, University of Washington Press

Semanário (Rio de Janeiro) September 26, 1963

Sen, Bhowani 1962 (1955), *Evolution of Agrarian Relations in India*, New Delhi, People's Publishing House

Simonsen, Roberto C. 1962, *Historia económica do Brasil* (1500-1820), Sao Paulo, Companhia Editora Nacional, 4 edicao

Sodré, Nelson Worneck, n.d. *Formacao histórica do Brasil*, Sao Paulo, Editora Brasiliense

Stavenhagen, Rodolfo 1969, *Las clases sociales en las sociedades agrarias*, México, Siglo XXI

Strachey, John 1959, *The End of Empire*, London, Victor Gollancz

Sunkel, Oswaldo Y Pedro Paz 1970, *El Subdesarrollo Latinoamericano y la Teoría del Desarrollo*, Mexico, Siglo XXI Editores

Time (International Edition) October 25, 1963

Vitale, Luis 1968-1969, *Interpretación Marxista de la Historia de Chile*, Santiago, Prensa Latinoamericana, Tomos I & II

Williams, Eric 1944, *Capitalism and Slavery*, Chapel Hill, University of North Carolina Press; reprinted, London, Andre Deutsch 1964 and New York, Citadel Press

Woddis, Jack 1960, *Africa: The Roots of Revolt*, New York, Citadel Press